"The Band of Sisters has embraced my first golden rule for changing the gamebook, enabling all women to finally succeed in the workplace. For all women to advance in the masculine-centered workplace, they must come together using their voices and energy to dismantle gender discriminatory systems brick by brick. These sisters have the proven grit, influence, and grace (GIG) to do just that! Their combined wisdom and proven actions for creating a cultural workplace where both women and men can thrive is truly invaluable."

Dr. Ella Bell—Professor of Management, Tuck School of Business. Author of *Our Separate Ways: Black and White Women and The Struggle for Professional Identity* (2001 and 2021); and *Career GPS: Strategies for Women Navigating the New Corporate Landscape*

"I applaud the focus on these micro-aggressions that many of us have learned to ignore but still get in the way of a fully inclusive workplace—time for these to be addressed once and for all."

Debra Sandler—Former President, Mars Chocolate North America, board member of multiple Fortune 100 Companies

"This book makes a seminal contribution to dismantling the remaining everyday gender bias that all too often still pervades the workplace. For aspiring women business executives, it contains invaluable practical tips to navigate the micro moments of gender bias with savvy while effectively advancing their career. For male executive allies, it is an eye opener into the often-unrealized slights women experience. This book is a must read for anyone trying to build a winning, more gender neutral, inclusive organization where everyone can realize their full potential to make a difference."

Mike White—Former CEO, DIRECTV

"*You Should Smile More* is a 'must read' that captures the many unfortunate situations that women of all backgrounds and experiences still encounter today during their ascension and arrival to the C-suite of organizations."

Ronald C. Parker—Former President & CEO, The Executive Leadership Council

"*You Should Smile More* is a must read for any executive that wants to make an impact and lead by example. It answers the questions you have and even the ones you didn't know you should have. The book is filled with real life examples of how to (and not to) get the most out of your teams."

Russell Weiner—Chief Operating Officer and President, Domino's US

HOW TO DISMANTLE
GENDER BIAS IN THE WORKPLACE

THE BAND OF SISTERS

who have seen it all, from the bottom rung to the boardroom:
Dawn Hudson, Angelique Bellmer Krembs, Katie Lacey,
Lori Tauber Marcus, Cie Nicholson, and Mitzi Short

CITY POINT PRESS 2022

Published by:

City Point Press

P.O. Box 2063

Westport CT 06880

(203) 571-0781

Cover and book design by Barbara Aronica-Buck

Cover image based on art by istock/kyoshino

Illustrations by Maxwell Schwear

Hardcover ISBN 978-1-947951-52-5

eBook ISBN 978-1-947951-53-2

Manufactured in the United States of America

CONTENTS

Why We Wrote This Book

A woman walks into a conference room for a meeting. Already at the table are two men, deep into a discussion of last night's football game. As more men enter, they join the sports talk. She's not a football fan. She waits patiently for the conversation to turn to business.

Colleagues are talking about a new, plum assignment that has come open. When a woman's name is mentioned, a man says: "Oh, she can't take it. She has two little kids."

It's Bagel Tuesday and the catered platters are wrapped and in the center of the conference table. Men enter the room, but nobody touches food. It's a Cellophane Standoff. It lingers until a woman arrives and unwraps the breakfast.

If you are a woman in any of these situations, you may be feeling a whiff of gender bias but not sure if or how to react. Or you could be a co-worker who witnesses a slight, and would like to be an ally. Or you're the boss and you came up in a time when all these issues were discussed and debated and supposedly addressed and all you can do is roll your eyes and think: *Really?!? Still?!?*

What can you do?

We are here to start a new conversation that answers that question. We are six C-suite women with a collective resume that covers twenty-nine industries, from large corporates to small start-ups, holding most every title through the C-suite including CEO, president, chief marketing officer and dozens of boards and advisory positions. We have seen it all, from the bottom rung to the boardroom. We are using our real-world experience to call on all rising leaders and allies to unlock a culture of greatness for women in the workforce—one little thing at a time.

You Should Smile More is a book about the workplace offenses many didn't know mattered. The small indignities, barriers, slights (many unconscious) that women face every day in the corporate workplace. They are not "#Metoo" moments. But they are not "nothing" either. They are the particles that collect around us and create barriers to our careers. They are the walls that go up, one grain of sand at a time. They are the moments that slow-build until the unwelcome environment takes hold and women disengage.

Ours is a guide—for women and for men—ready to take on the micro moments and advance women in the corporate workplace as equals. It is the how-to for dismantling everyday gender bias that continues to pervade the work world, from assumptions that keep us out of top jobs to corporate getaways that always seem to feature sports, to meetings at which women are the ones asked to take notes, to greetings where men are offered a handshake and women a hug.

We call ourselves the Band of Sisters—a name we gave ourselves after years of working together. We come to this teaching moment armed with a lifetime of experience and research. We six met over the course of a decade in various roles at PepsiCo. We've gotten to know each other well over the past twenty-five years. And in these pages, you'll get to know us, too.

Dawn Hudson

At Pepsi: President and CEO Pepsi-Cola North America; CEO PepsiCo Foodservice, CMO, Pepsi-Cola North America.

Post Pepsi: Vice-Chairman, Parthenon; CMO, National Football League (NFL).

Today: Board member: Nvidia, Interpublic Companies, and Rodan + Fields.

Angelique Bellmer Krembs

At Pepsi: VP Marketing, Pepsi US Beverages Portfolio; VP Marketing, Trademark Pepsi Brand.

Post Pepsi: CMO, News America Marketing; Fractional CMO to a portfolio of private equity-backed companies.

Recent: Managing Director, Global Head of Brand at BlackRock.

Katie Lacey

At Pepsi: VP Marketing, Carbonated Soft Drinks, VP Marketing, Colas and Media. Range of marketing roles at Pepsi-Cola and Frito-Lay.

Post Pepsi: President and CEO, Crane Stationery; SVP Marketing, ESPN.

Today: Board member: Designer Protein.

Lori Tauber Marcus

At Pepsi: SVP, Marketing Activation; SVP & General Manager, Global Customer Development.

Post Pepsi: CMO, The Children's Place Retail Stores; EVP, Keurig. Green Mountain; Interim Global CMO, Peloton Interactive.

Today: Board Member: Fresh Del Monte Produce (NYSE: FDP) and 24-Hour Fitness. Nonprofit board director: Multiple Myeloma

Research Foundation (MMRF) and Share Cancer Support. Advisor to early stage, direct-to-consumer companies and Executive Coach to C-suite executives.

Cie Nicholson

At Pepsi: CMO, Pepsi-Cola North America; VP Non-Carbonated Beverages, Pepsi-Cola North America.

Post Pepsi: CMO Equinox; CMO, Softcard; investor and advisor to several start-ups.

Today: Board Member, Selective Insurance Group (NASDAQ: SIGI); investor and advisor to several start-ups. Handstander: I am on a 20-year quest (2015-2035) to do handstands all over the world. Instagram-@cienicholson.

Mitzi Short

At Pepsi: VP & General Manager, PepsiCo Customer Team, VP, Multicultural Marketing, VP Customer Sales–West.

Post Pepsi: Co-Founder & Managing Partner, New Season Coaching & Consulting Group.

Today: CEO, New Season Coaching & Consulting Group; Franchise Owner, GOLFTEC; Board Member, Fund for Education Abroad.

We're your mentors on this journey. And we come to this job with a determined sense of purpose.

We navigated our own career trajectories and, as we rose into senior management, we mentored and supervised younger women. What's more, for the purposes of this book, the six of us set out on a listening tour to interview the next generation of women coming into the corporate ranks behind us. As we gathered our interviews and reviewed our findings, we were tempted to call this book "*Still?!?!*" in horrified recognition that so much of what we faced in the workplace remains true today. In too many workplaces, men continue to dominate discussions, meetings, and executive offices. They allow assumptions about women that permeate decisions around promotions and hiring. They give themselves and each other the benefit of the doubt while holding women to higher, often impossible, standards. For women of color, the bar is set even higher.

We also ran our findings by the men in our work lives. And many of them, when confronted with the situations that made us fume, truly had no idea there was a problem. This despite the fact that there are many more women in corporate America than was the case when we six first entered the workplace. Women now make up more than 45 percent of the U.S. workforce and 56 percent of college students. Two-thirds are white and one-third are women of color. The participation of women overall is equal to the EU and ahead of many Asian nations.

Turns out, that number is deceiving. Hiring more women was only the first step. Creating a culture that allows them to work to their full potential is pending. With the volume of women at work, we have achieved gender diversity. But we have not achieved inclusion.

In this book, you'll find easy-to-access sections. We see our readers in three categories: women who want to make changes in their own work experiences; leaders who want to create inclusive workplaces; and witnesses—those who would like to be allies to women in the workplace. We want you to be able to say something when you see something.

We will present readers with a situation and then offer our take on how it might be addressed. We represent a range of tactical approaches. Some of us are more direct, others are more subtle. Readers will be able to see for themselves which option works for them. In addition to our advice, we will offer the research of experts in the field who show how lingering gender bias is in fact a problem in the workplace—one that limits women in their advancement and companies in their quest for best talent.

We have organized our book into sections, each of which identifies a sphere in which things go sideways for women in the workplace—from conversations, to hiring and promotion discussions, and even in afterwork drinks. Under the heading of each section, we provide short chapters that state the specific problem, share stories of our experiences, and offer concrete solutions.

We're writing this book as part of a larger business launch we call *The Band of Sisters*—a consultancy dedicated to facing down the issue of gender bias in the workplace.

The lingering of gender bias—conscious or not—in the corporate world hurts us all. A company's culture is stimulated by the ideas, customs, and social behaviors of its individuals. When company values and behaviors aren't taking advantage of the diversity of thinking from all levels of the organization, they risk not optimizing the people they've hired. They risk devaluing their sense of importance. They risk disengaging employees and creating a poor work culture. Allowing women and all diverse people to realize their full potential is good for companies. Diversity breeds better solutions faster *if* people feel comfortable to freely express themselves and are comfortable in their environment.

In the business world, barriers to inclusion are barriers to success.

Women have lived through the battles around lawsuits and legislation. We have been part of the evolution of corporate diversity statements and public proclamations. We're at the point now where we, all of us, around conference tables and water coolers and Zoom meetings, must make the final push for change. We are not here to attack. We are experienced leaders and we are here to spark new conversations that will lead to the behavioral changes necessary to bring about more diverse, equitable, and inclusive cultures.

Here's how.

Section One

When They Say . . .

Often the biggest hurdles to women occur in casual conversation in the workplace. These are not official communications. Instead, they are the chatter of the day. They're what we say to each other in the hall, in the cafeteria, in the conference room before the meeting starts. The casual setting may lead us to take these moments lightly. But in fact, they create a tone and a framework that sets women at a disadvantage.

CHAPTER 1

Who's the New Girl?

How to handle casual sexist language

Did you meet the new girl in accounting?"

"Thanks, dear."

"Well, isn't she feisty!"

The language is so casual, so prevalent, that you may hardly notice it. It's a diminutive, a tiny word, dropped into the sea of discussion that flows through an office daily. Compared to the work to be done, the challenges to be faced, those words seem small.

Most days, you may not even notice them.

Gender-biased wording is so pervasive, pushing it back may seem like embracing air. How many times a day do you hear a man use a term of endearment in conversation with a female colleague? How many times does a man use "girl" to describe a grown woman?

How often do you care?

It's a fair question. When held up against other issues—unequal pay, unwanted touching, lack of leadership opportunities—casual sexist language seems like a low value target. Certainly, our media is full of the word "girl" and it's often used in positive ways—*You go, girl!* Who really cares if a guy calls you "honey" or the men refer to female colleagues as girls?

But we open our book on improving culture with this topic because with their very smallness, these words make our larger point. These tiny, seemingly insignificant words are exactly what we're talking about. "Girl" is just one example. These words are what make up the smallest particles of the workplace. Individually, they are negligible. But every day, everywhere, for years, they begin to cling together, forming a larger whole. Small words alone aren't harmful. It's their mass that makes them worrisome. When you hear them over years, they form a background noise you come to accept. They create an atmosphere that everyone—men and women—seems to embrace as okay. When the little words flow freely, the bigger barriers are eventually formed. Words matter. Men who think of their female colleagues as girls will hardly be accepting of them as CEO.

We have noticed it in different ways. Sometimes, it's subtle.

"The word 'girl' is said every day in the workplace," notes Cie. "Girl is the term for a female child or adolescent. The word 'woman' is a term for an adult. People don't call a grown man a boy. It would be very odd to hear someone say we just hired a boy from Yale. When a group of adult women are dismissed as a bunch of 'girls,' it feels to me like we're being talked down to in a condescending way."

Sometimes, the word hits with a bang, as it did one day for Angelique.

I have to admit, I didn't think this was a big deal. I hadn't remembered or noticed anyone addressing a woman as "girl," though I was sure that if it happened, I would just calmly correct the offender and say: "You mean woman." But then it happened—a man in a small meeting said, "I know an expert we can bring in on this topic, there is a girl in the data department who would be great." He was referring to an award-winning scientist. And guess what —I froze. Said nothing. It just went by. After the session, the only other woman in the meeting said, "I can't believe that happened! He called this award-winning scientist a GIRL!" I'm sure that man has no idea how much the two women in that meeting are still thinking about that fleeting comment.

The language issue shows no sign of abatement. When we interviewed women in the generation that followed us into the workplace, we heard similar tales. One woman, a veterinarian in her thirties, told us that people routinely forget to use her title. People address her male colleagues as Dr. Smith and Dr. Jones, but call her, instead, by her first name. She also noticed that when people do remember to use the "doctor" salutation, they often call her "Dr. Jane" instead of using her last name.

The wording does more than make us flinch. Research suggests that language is a brick in the wall—an element of everyday work that maintains a status quo of male power. A study conducted by a team from the University of Waterloo and Duke University reported "gendered wording" is an often unacknowledged way a company maintains institutional inequality.

In other words, words are part of the larger problem. They are used to keep inequality in place.

It's not just casual conversation. Sexist language is part of the larger infrastructure of many work cultures. A study from Walden University in Minnesota looked at the letters of recommendation drafted for women versus men. The letters for men used what researchers call "agentic" terms—words that convey agency and leadership. Examples: superb, excellent, assertive, dominant, strong, problem solver. The letters for women, on the other hand, used more "communal" terms such as sympathetic, thoughtful, calm, and friendly.

What do those word choices say to you?

Deb Liu, a Silicon Valley executive, began compiling an interesting list during her time at Facebook. She began collecting male and female words or phrases she heard around the office—sometimes even from her own mouth. In the "male" column she listed things like Man Up, Ballsy, Gentlemen's Agreement, and Manpower. In the "female column" were Run Like a Girl, Debbie Downer, and Diva.

Even popular phrases in tech research came with gender baggage. "Two guys in a garage" was slang for startup. And "would your mom be able to use this product?" was the standard benchmark for vetting an innovation—mom being the lowest common denominator of users. "What surprised me was how deep our gender-specific language runs," Liu wrote in her essay on the topic. "These words were not said with misogynistic or negative intent, but rather they were used in apparently innocuous ways."

And then there are the words that everyone knows are criticisms directed only at women: feisty, bossy, pushy, high maintenance, bitch.

Words matter.

Whether obviously hurtful or seemingly innocuous, words set the stage for the way women are treated. Titles and labels formed the basis for a South Korean study of gender-biased language in the workplace. The study published in 2020 found words like freshman and chairman continue to pervade the academic world and are part of the "non-parallel treatment" afforded women and men in academia.

There's even sexism in words that are left out. Consider the controversy started when an op-ed in the *Wall Street Journal* suggested First Lady Jill Biden not use her academic title—doctor—because she was not a medical doctor. Douglas Emhoff, husband of Vice President Kamala Harris posted on Twitter: "This story would never have been written about a man."

Indeed, Amy Diehl and Leanne Dzubinski, both PhDs, proposed a term for this: *Untitling*. This is the practice of omitting titles when referring to women, while still using them for men. It's a practice that diminishes women's authority and credibility, they write.

The problem is that pointing out sexist language in a document, such as a job posting or a letter of recommendation, is relatively easy— at least compared to the daunting task of dealing with the issue in the midst of a conversation. Even women who would feel comfortable circling an offending term and showing it to the author might balk at the notion of interrupting someone in mid-sentence.

That's the reason casual sexist language often gets a pass.

How do we address this? What can we do about sexist language?

If it's you . . .

When you hear it, try Cie's strategy:

> I try to handle this situation in a friendly and non-combative way. I often repeat someone's exact sentence substituting the word woman for girl. So, when they say: "There is a new girl who just started in accounting." I repeat back: "There is a new *woman* who just started in accounting" and then I smile to emphasize the point as gentle feedback. I find when I do this two to three times to an individual, they start catching themselves.

Mitzi advocates for a direct approach. No need to sugar coat the obvious, she says. When you hear it, say: "There are no girls in the workplace." How you say it matters. Tailor your language to the audience. Some appreciate hearing it straight and others may need a more nuanced conversation. But calling out the language in the moment makes a powerful statement.

Katie has an additional take on this issue—one that suggests men are not the only ones in need of a language update:

> I've heard women be the offenders of this one too! It's startling and I usually don't hear what someone says right after it. We should make sure that we are not using the term ourselves. When we interviewed younger women, they told us that they often used the term "girl." When using with peers it may seem normal and natural—continuing a term they have used most of their life when they were indeed girls. Where it becomes more awkward is when older and more senior men use the term which can, intentionally or not, call out females in a demeaning light as someone not as substantial or not taken as seriously.

As we correct their language, we need to also correct our own.

If you're the boss . . .
Cie says:

> I ask them to repeat what they just said but substitute boy for girl. Ninety-five percent of the time it is impossible for someone to say, "There is a new boy who just started in

accounting" without laughing. The laughter lightens the mood and emphasizes my point.

Lori takes the gentle correction strategy and raises it to a teaching moment.

I like to really expand it. Try this, "Oh when you said, 'GIRL,' I got distracted. You mean, Allison, the new *woman* in accounting. Yes. She's excellent. She recently joined us from XYZ company, and I think her knowledge of working with founders in post-IPO companies is going to be really useful. I've already been in a few meetings with her where I've been so impressed by her extensive knowledge of securities law.

If you're the witness . . .

The casual use of sexist language is an opportunity for everyone to participate in the evolution of the company culture. Says Mitzi: "This is where allies can play a role 'correcting' the use of words like 'girl,' when they hear them and by role modeling more inclusive behavior."

CHAPTER 2

Father of the Year

When working moms are criticized
and working dads get a trophy

There are many topics for which society sorts men and women into different buckets, but none more polarizing than family responsibilities. Even as we discuss "having it all" and women in leadership roles, when it comes to family—and most of the time when we say family, we mean children—men and women get very different signals.

A survey by Pew Research shows the split:

When asked to name the ideal situation for young children, the vast majority of respondents said they should have a mom who worked part-time or didn't work at all. Only 16 percent said a full-time working mom was ideal.

When asked to describe the ideal situation for *the mom* in that scenario, respondents went even harder on the part-time option—47 percent said that was the ideal situation for mom. The same 33 percent said mom should be at home full time. And now, only 12 percent thought mom should hold a full-time job.

Then Pew flipped the question: What's the ideal situation for *a dad* with young children? It wasn't even close. Seventy percent said he should be working full time.

The message in this study could not be more vivid: women with small children should not work full time—it's best for everyone, mom and kids alike.

It's under this vivid expression of public opinion and experience that women try to move ahead in corporate workplaces. They are juggling work and family responsibilities in the full knowledge that survey after survey thinks they should be spending more time at home.

That's hard enough to manage, but in recent years, we see a new trend moving into this discussion: the involved dad.

And who can be critical of that? Dads are shrugging off the 1950s image as breadwinners disengaged from the daily lives of their offspring. They are taking time to show up at soccer games, be home for dinner, and devote time to their families. They are reaching out and claiming their right to be more than a paycheck in the family ecosystem. They are embracing their roles as warm-blooded caretakers.

All great. Until you swivel the spotlight back to the office and find that while men are getting accolades for their efforts (and again, that's a positive trend), women are still struggling under a torrent of negativity—and it's coming from all fronts—the boss, colleagues, and that nagging inner critic that tells working mothers they are never, ever going to be enough.

This is not a relic of the mid-twentieth century, when a woman in the workplace was a new idea. This split, in which men are praised for their childcare efforts and women are dinged for the same behavior, is going on now.

We had no difficulty sourcing stories from our younger workplace sisters on this topic. Here's one of their takes:

One summer, there was a man in the office who made a commitment to be at his son's swim lessons. The lesson was in the middle of the week, in the middle of the day, around 2:00 p.m. So, all summer, this man was gone Wednesdays, midday to be at his son's swim lesson. He usually didn't come back in and just finished up from home. Everyone was so positive about it. He's at the swim lesson *and* presenting the next day! What a great dad! And I had to think: Women do that every day. How do you talk about the woman who has left early for family reasons?

There's no medal for that, she noted.

And here's another, featuring one of our younger colleagues now watching a woman and a man juggle the same responsibility.

I was in a meeting that ran late. Present at that meeting were two similarly ranked individuals—one man and one woman. As the meeting ticked past 5:00 p.m., the woman leaned over to me and said: "I'm so sorry, I have to leave to pick up my daughter. Would you mind taking notes for me?" I said, sure, no problem. As the woman left, she apologized over and over as she went out the door. "I'm so sorry." Even that night, when she logged on to her email to read my notes and follow up, she was still carrying that, still apologizing for having to leave to get her child.

About a week later, there was a similarly important meeting with the same attendees. The man I mentioned sent an email around: "Wife is out of town so I'm on pick up duty. I won't be at the meeting. Thanks."

And that was it. Just: Thanks. No "I'm so sorry." No "please take notes." Just: "I won't be there because I have a family obligation."

The difference in tone was stark, she said. The man simply made his availability known. The woman felt the need to apologize. The split in psychological safety is apparent. Women believe they are judged and miss out on opportunities for development and growth because of assumptions made about their ability or willingness to navigate childcare. They hide it or downplay it. For women who can't afford nannies or *au pairs* or after-school support, this is a constant threat. Men don't experience this sense of danger and so revealing a childcare responsibility is not a risk.

There are many ways business must act to support working mothers, but this is the split screen—the different way moms and dads are viewed—that we'll bring into focus here. This is the place in which the culture mandate is clear. We need to acknowledge that workplaces judge moms and dads differently—and that many times dads get a halo while moms get a side-eye.

We saw that routinely in our work.

"There no doubt is a double standard for women handling family challenges in the workforce. Expect an eye roll when Jane has to leave to pick up her sick child from school versus accolades and admiration if Jeff has to do the same task," says Cie.

And as leaders, we see that pressure persists, even as technology like Zoom should allow us more flexibility to handle family responsibilities. Dawn saw this during the COVID pandemic: "Most people who were able to keep their jobs had to work from home and without childcare. If a man was on a Zoom call and a child interrupted the screen, people would say: *Aw, how nice. Isn't that cute?* But I am on a board with a female CEO whose husband works and has two girls under ten at home without childcare. She chose to venture into the office to avoid a child meltdown while on Zoom. I encouraged her to do the calls from home and we would applaud her as she juggled. But she feared the double standard."

And is she wrong? When a woman has a childcare issue, it's because she failed to properly manage her work and family responsibilities. She dropped the ball. The comments around the office are all about how she was unable to get childcare coverage. But when a man juggles family care, he often gets a different reaction. He's an involved dad. He's making time for his kids. He's forging a new path for working fathers.

Part of the problem may simply be volume. For women, demands of family are more chronic, rather than acute. One missed meeting, one early exit has little impact on a woman's career. But since the bulk of family responsibility falls to women, the challenge of managing both work and home life is routine. Indeed, a woman with young children or elderly parents may find this conflict crops up on a regular basis. During the COVID-19 shutdown, this reality exploded. Women found themselves at home, trying to do their jobs, homeschool their children, and safeguard a wide swath of relatives from the virus. Their ongoing family responsibilities were visible in their Zoom screens. And even as offices reopened, if one time someone in the office says, "Jessica couldn't get kid coverage," and rolls his eyes, there's little impact. If that happens routinely, the eye roll is going to build into a problematic reputation. Women are hurt by the collective impression that they're routinely compromised by family demands. It's the cumulative effects of this reaction that become a drag on a woman's advancement.

Meanwhile the dads, with their less frequent family-related absences, get a boost for their efforts.

Still, it is a split in treatment that calls for a culture change.

How to handle:

If it's you . . .

If family responsibilities take you away from work, avoid the impression of apology. It serves to reinforce the idea that somehow, as a woman with a family issue, you are making a mistake. Instead, take a cue from the dads and be clear and unemotional with your information. As one senior woman put it: decide to be where you are. When you're at work, be at work. If you are at home, be at home. Don't let the pull of the other place distract you. Part of the reason workplaces react badly is that women telegraph their own sense of discomfort when work and family issues collide.

This was Lori's strategy. And, she concedes, it was a work in constant progress.

> I worked full time in a dual-career marriage for the majority of my children's lives. There were times I missed things that I didn't want to miss (like being away at work when college acceptance letters came . . . or, worse yet, being away when college rejection letters came) or having to leave things early (like the day we moved into our house, when I was six months pregnant with my second child and as I was getting ready mid-day to fly to Dallas for a big meeting, my two-year-old touched my big belly and asked me to explain where babies come from!). I tortured myself for a while and then I finally worked out a system. It involves managing others and managing myself.
>
> In terms of managing others, I agree with what was said above—be brief. Less is more. Say, "I'm unable to make the 8:00 a.m. meeting; I have an appointment outside the office;

I can dial in any time after 10:15 or can be here in person by 11:00 a.m." Enough said. Managing my own "crap" (that's a technical term for a combination of guilt, imposter syndrome, and fear of failure at both work and home) was harder. What finally worked for me was to create some rules of the road for each phase of my life. When my children were younger, I made peace with the fact that I would be there in the mornings (not usually leaving for work until almost 8:00 a.m.), but I was rarely home for early dinners. I made peace that I would not be able to volunteer at the school office, but I would never miss the Halloween parade at the elementary school. I set expectations accordingly with my husband and my daughters, and it helped me push away all the loud, disruptive noises in my head.

The next generation of women in the workforce say they often give no explanation. Less is more, said one. "If someone asks if I can attend the 8:00 meeting, I say: Unfortunately, that doesn't work for me. Please suggest another time. Sometimes I just say no. After all, 'No' is a complete sentence."

If you're the boss . . .

Demonstrate and articulate support for the work/family juggle. That's important for all team members, but it may take some repetition for women to internalize. Senior women need to say to each other and to their direct reports that family balance is nothing to be ashamed of. "Men and women in the workplace should work extra hard to reinforce great parental behavior equally for women and men and acknowledge that raising children with the demands of a job is hard and no one is perfect," says Dawn.

Mitzi offers this idea for managers:

> One of my coaching clients shared how she manages this: she sets and maintains boundaries during evenings and she protects the 6–8 p.m. time frame for her family. We eat together, spend time together, then I bathe the kids and put them to bed. After 8 p.m./bedtime, if I need to be on a call or to work on a project or attend to email, I do. Wouldn't it be great if the 6–8 p.m. hours were "off limits" automatically for companies and organizations? Then no one would feel left out or put out—men or women.

Katie suggests managers check themselves when it comes to worrying about the family responsibilities of team members.

> Don't ask women "who's watching the kids?" when they are working late, traveling, etc., if you are not asking men the same question. A male colleague once told me that he caught himself about to ask a female colleague how her husband was doing watching the kids during a weekend work event when she was away all weekend but realized he would never ask a male colleague that question, so luckily stopped himself.

If you're the witness . . .

Make an effort to applaud the women as often as you applaud the men. Men often get accolades for a single act of childcare (and women are often the most vocal in their praise), whereas women get little applause for their everyday heroics.

Katie's take:

It's a great aspect of recent history that men are more involved in their children's lives and activities than men of previous generations. Dads are coaching their daughter's soccer teams, going to parent-teacher conferences and doing school drop-offs. And much like when they emptied the dishwasher that one time, somehow the thing that women do every day without acclaim is now a thing to be celebrated and remarked upon. I believe that we have the bar a little too low for men. If you're not commenting about how great Allison is because she is going to her kid's little league game, then don't spend ten minutes talking about what a great dad Dan is because he did. Let's have a consistent bar across the board.

A good way to address this is to be aware and find a gentle way to point it out when you see it happening. Balancing families and careers is difficult for both genders, but keep an eye out for where we are celebrating the one thing for men that we hold a woman back for.

Even if the mom is making it look easy and the dad is making it look like he's just climbed Mount Everest, acknowledge all parents in their efforts equally. See it as part of your responsibility to shift the conversation around work/family issues.

CHAPTER 3

You Should Smile More

Why female facial expressions end up in annual reviews

I t's valid to explore why women should be asked to smile at all, in any setting. But for our purposes, let's address the office locale.

The smile demand is real. Some of us have it in writing.

For Katie, the suggestion that she smile more emerged in her annual review. She'd moved to a new company, in a senior role. "I was told that I needed to smile more and greet people when I walked down the halls," she said. Upon further investigation, she discovered this meant the many people who worked in the low-walled cubicles in other departments of the company. Since Katie was new, these were mostly people she did not yet know. The critique struck her as odd. But she realized immediately it could affect her ability to do her job. "I ran straight into the trap that women can't be both competent and warm. I think that many people view a woman in charge as cold and unapproachable, so anything you do to reinforce that view can get traction. I am fairly certain that no man has ever been told he needs to smile more," she said.

For Mitzi, the smile issue was raised in a more casual way. "Early in my career, I can recall being asked: "What's wrong?" Or told: "You look so serious!" If I followed up on the reason for the inquiry I heard: "It's because you aren't smiling." Since I am usually smiling and upbeat,

I responded: 'Thanks for the feedback' and made a mental note about the importance of non-verbal behaviors and assumptions." But even when the smile issue was raised in a concerned way, Mitzi was aware of the damage labels could do to one's career—especially, the Angry Black Woman. "The question left me curious about what assumptions and judgments people make about smiling, not smiling, and other non-verbal cues."

Just recently, working as an executive coach, Mitzi faced the smile issue again, through the lens of a client. "An African American woman who works for a large firm said to me: "I've been told I need to smile more. Did anyone ever tell you that?" And in our discussion the issue surfaced: Are men asked to smile more? Why would someone try to dictate how I feel? What are the consequences of not smiling more? Why are so many women being told to smile?"

Not just decades ago. Now. Still.

To add insult to injury, smiling can even be used against you. Lori was never told to smile more. In fact, she got the opposite critique. "The advice I received was that I'm too friendly, too accessible, and that I needed to put up more barriers to be taken seriously."

The Millennials and Gen Zers we interviewed said smiling is still an issue in the workplace—although it's not always named as such. Said one: "In my review, my manager told me I was very calm and that could come off as lack of engagement. So, I've been working on my engagement—looking people in the eye, nodding more, having a smile on my face." The instruction wasn't specifically to smile, she said, but to have a more pleasing, engaging presence. The smile is part of that, she said.

To grin or not to grin? How should we deal with this?

The smile demand is one that doesn't offer a clear mandate. Women have decidedly split reactions. For some, the issue of smiling in the workplace is akin to dressing appropriately or wearing makeup. It's just part of building a successful personal brand. For others, the demand that women smile is demeaning. The comment is, at best, old-fashioned, and, at worst, harassment. Smiles—and requests for more of them—are a complicated topic.

Interestingly, a woman's smile was not always considered a positive trait. Writer J. R. Thorpe covered this history in her article for *Bustle*: In the Middle Ages, Thorpe noted, smiling was considered low-class, or even dangerous. At least one critic of da Vinci's masterpiece, *The Mona Lisa*, criticized the subject's smile as aggressive and possibly malevolent. Women who smiled were not to be trusted.

Some polite smiling (no teeth!) became more acceptable as the centuries wore on, but cultural observers note the elevation of a woman's smile truly emerged in the twentieth century, with the rise of American advertising. Now, a woman's grin was a sales tool. It launched innovations. It was a key feature in ads for home goods such as washing machines and cookware. The best, most effective ads featured the glamorous—smiling—housewife.

When women entered the workplace, the smile issue followed them. Industries that welcomed women were those in which a smile was an asset, even a requirement—nursing, teaching, shop clerks, secretaries. For this wave of working women, a pretty smile was part of the job. The women who displayed it were rewarded for it.

But in the corporate workplace, smiling became a flashpoint. Women (not men) were asked to smile more to appear approachable, less threatening. Women (not men) were complimented for smiling, as if they were present as decoration, rather than equal participants. The absence of a smile on a woman's face was read as aggressive, adversarial, and as Mitzi put it, angry. This, even though research indicates men and women in the workplace actually smile in equal amounts. A study by Marianne LaFrance, a professor of psychology at Yale University, set out to quantify the smile factor. She found that while overall, women smile slightly more often than men, in power settings, they are nearly equal. Men and women smile at about the same rate when they are in the same positions of power, occupation, and social role. That suggests that Katie was smiling at about the same rate as her male counterparts, but they weren't being asked to look warmer and more approachable as they walked past the cubicles. Only she got that note.

The demand to smile more continues into the current work generation, although under a new heading. Now, instead of "smile more" younger women in the workplace are more likely to be warned that they have a "resting bitch face." In 2015, the *New York Times* wrote a trend piece on the topic. Headline: "I'm Not Mad. That's Just My RBF." Country singer Kasey Musgraves once commented a more accurate name for RBF might be "This Wouldn't Bother You If I Was a Guy" Face.

The language has evolved but the demand that women adjust their facial muscles to convey warmth and compliance has not. This is not just a critique from the patriarchy. Women will often level this charge at each other. RBF is not a compliment.

The smile issue is one gaining traction in the social world as more women describe it as a catcall or harassment. Street murals that read "Stop telling women to smile!" have appeared in major cities. Increasingly, the "Smile, honey!" line is associated with older men who have missed the shifting social current.

One of our younger colleagues told us smiling—when to and how much—remains an issue in the workplace:

This is an interesting question for me. I am naturally a person who smiles a lot, so I don't often get told that I need to smile more, but instead get comments on my smile. I specifically remember one instance a few months ago where I did a Zoom meeting with one of our older male clients. Prior to the meeting, I had only spoken to him on the phone a few years before. Apparently, he hadn't liked me because he thought I was too pushy. However, when he saw me in this Zoom presentation, we finished and he commented on how great my smile was, then later told my colleague who now sells to him that he liked me much more.

I also had a stint where I tried not smiling. As a person who smiles a lot, people would see me smiling and young and take me less seriously. I have a friend who told me that she never smiled at work. She was head of construction of a restaurant and said that she went into one meeting, happy and smiling, and after that her boss told her that she'd go a longer way without smiling. So, she stopped smiling. I decided to try it, too, and immediately ran into many walls. People can't put together someone like me not smiling and they ask why I look so upset if I'm not smiling (with just a normal face). It's a lot of pressure, to always have to be happy or positive, and if I'm not, people will comment and draw away. This wasn't great for sales, so I returned to smiling, which is usually a natural state, so doesn't usually feel forced. *But* it does really upset me that if I don't smile or am serious, I get a negative reaction (people think I'm being emotional?!). I don't have the freedom to be who I am in the moment.

Said another rising leader we interviewed: "In my opinion, 'smile more' doesn't typically come from a constructive place, but from a 'you need to change yourself so I'm less intimidated and more comfortable' place."

But the RFB discussion suggests the issue is not laid to rest entirely, and particularly in the workplace, where issues of power and competition remain.

How should you handle the demand to smile more?

If it's you . . .

Get more detail. When you're in a review or mentoring situation, face the smiling issue head on, says Lori: "If they say you don't smile enough, say, 'Can you elaborate on that? I don't smile enough compared to whom?' You can also assume positive intent and assume there is something productive in the feedback. Try saying, 'Can you please give me an example of that behavior? When you saw it and what its impact was on the situation.' Sometimes you'll find out you may have some blind spots tracking your impact on others. When that's not the case, the person giving you this feedback will be forced to think through the impact of your actions."

You may also be able to demonstrate that your lack of smile isn't actually a critical business issue. "Get the other person talking about it. Say something like, 'I'm super focused and fully present during meetings/Zoom calls. I make it my business to really lean forward and focus on the topic at hand. Tell me more about what you're not seeing.' A non-defensive tone can help the commenting person to realize there may not be much substance behind their criticism.

Get to the bottom of the matter. You may also want to try to decode the comment. "I think that the 'you don't smile enough' comment can be code for 'people are intimidated and/or scared of you,'" says Katie. If you're in a senior position, you may want to decide if this criticism matters to you. "For whatever reason, we typically don't worry about men in leadership positions being intimidating. As a woman, I would say that you can decide whether this is a problem or not for you. If you want to be perceived as less intimidating, then create informal, personal situations with people where you can counter that perception. Bring your dog to work, host a pizza party for your team, have your group over for a backyard barbecue—all of those present a more personal side."

If you're not senior, Katie says, the smile comment may have a different meaning altogether. "If it's your boss telling you this, then it's probably code for: you seem hostile or unhappy. In that case, reassure them that you are happy (if you are) and that perhaps you just tend to furrow your brow when you are thinking and then try and practice having a more open or neutral expression when you are concentrating."

Ultimately, it pays to remember that this is the workplace and you don't need to be everyone's best friend, she says. Assess this feedback and decide whether it's something you need to concern yourself with. It may not be.

Seize the opportunity. Remember that the smile comment may be an opening for you to express yourself. Mitzi points this out. "The other side of this discussion is that maybe a smile is not warranted. Maybe something was said or done that was disappointing or inappropriate. In that case, I need to say: 'I'm not smiling because I was disappointed in what I heard. And here's why.' It's an opportunity to open up a conversation about intent versus impact."

Some may prefer humor. "In the right crowd, you can come back with: "Oh, let me just put my smile on," says Mitzi. Cie also tries a humorous response. "In some situations, you can jokingly call it out:

"Isn't it interesting that you never tell Bob, John, or Sam to smile more? Or is it possible that some men don't also have resting bitch faces?"

If you're the boss . . .

Watch reviews carefully for the smiling issue. Are women being judged on this while men get a pass? What are reviewers trying to communicate when they raise the smiling issue? Dig into the issue to excavate the reasons behind the critique. Look for ways to expose the issue when it's underlying sexism and to translate it when it's valid advice that's been wrapped in a sexist trope.

As a leader in the workplace, you can also look for teaching moments. "Use the opportunity when someone says, 'Chuck is so friendly and always has a big smile on his face' to make the point: "Isn't it interesting, that is not often said when a woman is always smiling. In fact, sometimes we don't take her as seriously."

If you're the witness . . .

Don't participate in the snub. If everyone around the office says the new woman in senior management has a Resting Bitch Face, call that out as a throwback. Why do we ask women to smile? Why are we threatened when they don't? Open the conversation to air out the issue. "One consideration is that people have good days and bad days, smiley days and not so smiley days," says Mitzi. "Is there a pattern? Is the smiling/not smiling having an impact on the individual or those on the other end? Is this a difference that makes a difference? If the answer is *no*, maybe it's an observation that we don't need to act on."

CHAPTER 4

Susan, Will You Take Notes?

Administrative chores and gender bias

It's called "office housework."

Researchers Joan C. Williams and Marina Multhaup made the distinction in their article for *Harvard Business Review*. There are two kinds of work in most office environments. There's the "glamour work"—that's the kind of assignment that gets you noticed by the boss. Perhaps it's a project for a major client or the chance to build out a new team or the opportunity to represent the company at an industry conference.

Then, there's the flip side of that coin. These are the tasks that have to be done, but offer little or no chance to shine. These can be note-taking during a meeting, securing the conference room for a meeting, getting everyone onto a conference call or sending meeting invites. During the meeting it can be getting everyone dialed in or finding someone from IT to help with a tech problem. All are important to the smooth running of any office. But they're hardly a stepping-stone to greater things. For this reason, Williams and Multhaup call these tasks "office housework." Necessary, but decidedly unglamorous.

Let's pause a moment to make clear that these tasks are often performed by administrative assistants. In that context, we have no complaints. Indeed, great admins keep a great company running.

Without them, offices would spiral into chaos and conference room times would be determined by hand-to-hand combat. The issue with office housework is not the value of the tasks, but the way in which the tasks are distributed. When they're distributed to administrative assistants—whether male or female—that's fully appropriate and part of the job description. It's when there's no admin handy that things get problematic.

In a setting in which men and women of equal professional stature are present, women are often the ones tasked with the office house-work. What's more, women of color are more often saddled with this work than white women. Williams and Multhaup did specific research into the fields of engineering and law. In a survey of over 3,000 engineers, women overall were 29 percent more likely to report doing more office housework than their colleagues. When looking at the legal field, the researchers found women reported doing more office housework than men—again by double digits. Women of color reported that in addition to tasks like note-taking, they were more likely to handle tasks such as cleaning up coffee cups.

In the same surveys, both female engineers and lawyers reported they had less access to glamour work such as high-profile projects.

And this is why office housework matters. While it may seem like no big deal to take the notes or send invites for the next meeting, it's time a woman takes from her workday. A man can use those same few minutes to advance his own work. The problem with always being the one to take notes is that the note-taker is naturally less able to participate in the meeting. That's true of any housework task—when you're doing that, you're not doing something else. But the men are. You're busy with the notes, so you're not speaking up in the meet-ing, you're busy distributing notes or sending out the invites so you're not participating in post-meeting conversations in the hall. It also subtly or subliminally communicates that you or your role are not as important. The note-taker can become invisible.

We noticed this in our work.

"I didn't want it assumed that I would be taking, preparing, and distributing the notes all of the time. There's nothing wrong with taking notes if that's part of your job description. But if it isn't your job, that's a different story. Early in my career, I felt the risk of being miscast was fairly high," says Mitzi. "In addition, I felt if I had to worry about capturing all the comments and action items for everyone, I would be less able to stay present and fully engage in the discussion."

Women as note-takers was so prevalent, even women seemed to take it as a given.

"I can't count the number of times in team meetings or brainstorming sessions that a woman was the one asked to take the notes. And in some cases, if a female was not specifically asked to be the note-taker—a woman would volunteer out of habit or was the first to feel compelled to volunteer when the boss asked the group and no one else stepped up," says Cie. "So, there are many paths to get there, but in most cases the note-taker was a woman. It might not have always been me, but usually it was a woman."

Avoiding this trap is often a function of pointing out that there are others in the office who are paid to do the office housework. One of the rising leaders we interviewed uses this tactic. If she's asked to take notes, she has a prepared response: "I really want to be fully present and participate enthusiastically in this meeting. I won't be able to do that if I'm focused on taking notes. Let's bring in a more junior person to take the notes, who will learn a lot by experiencing this conversation with a senior group."

To be sure, note-taking isn't in and of itself a problematic task. In fact, it can be spun to great advantage.

Katie has seen that opportunity emerge.

> In certain meetings and situations, the note-taker can turn it into an advantage. If you happen to be someone who takes decent notes and is a good writer, the very exercise of doing it probably means you will have a better memory of a discussion and a better sense of what should happen from the meeting. Over time, that could broaden your perspective and get you noticed—and it could get you included in more important meetings and give you insight into other areas of the company. As the author, you can sometimes shape how something is recounted. I know that I would try and volunteer to write something up after an important discussion so that I would be a part of it and hopefully be in the room for any future discussions.

Angelique agrees:

> While simply recording the minutes is a junior task, there can be great power in "holding the pen" when a group's work gets summarized and circulated. I found that often the person who is the "deck master" or memo writer is also the one determining which comments get included and which do not. As a more junior person, this can get you included in more senior conversations, which is great for visibility and impact. Either way, the impact is still measured by how well you actively listen and produce an effective representation of the discussion, but there is definitely power in shaping the playback.

One of our younger interviewees has embraced this thinking—
with a caveat. If you're the note-taker, think about what you can
do with that material besides type it up. Here's how one of younger
colleagues handled the request that she take notes when she joined a
new team:

> I was put on a global team. I was so young and brand new
> to the company so it was really an honor to be in this group.
> Everybody in the room was two or three levels higher than
> me. I took on the responsibility of organizing the strategy and
> building the structure around it. So, this experience wasn't just
> about taking notes. It led to a promotion for me and job secu-
> rity during the recession.

But while the occasional office housekeeping can be leveraged, a
constant stream of these tasks holds women back.

What to do:

If it's you . . .

Suggest that the housework chore, whatever it is, be rotated.
"When an Administrative Assistant was not available to take notes, I
would proactively suggest that the note-taking duties rotate among the
participants," says Mitzi.

Lori takes the rotation suggestion a step further, embracing the
power of the note-taker to put the rotation of all housework into gear.

> First, if it's an ongoing meeting that happens each week,
> then when you publish the meeting minutes, pass the baton
> at the bottom of the notes and say "next week's notes will be

taken by Jimmy." Start the tradition that it rotates and use the actual notes to memorialize that idea. Alternatively (because I do believe that she who takes the notes controls what is memorialized for the meeting!), agree to take the notes and then say "I'm happy to take the notes. Let's divide up the other jobs: John, would you be in charge of ordering breakfast for the meeting each week? Carla, would you please be the time-keeper and keep us on agenda and on task? Jack, would you please be responsible for setting up the follow-up meetings with our key stakeholders after every meeting and making sure we have the PowerPoint to use in those meetings?" By spreading the work around, you no longer seem subservient.

Finally, consider whether taking notes can be turned to your advantage. While you may want to avoid being the go-to note-taker, it's smart to notice when the process helps you.

If you're the boss . . .

Take a page from Richard Branson's playbook. He is a big pro-ponent of note-taking on a personal level. But he also recognizes the way the chore often falls to women—a practice he says hurts everyone. "Not only is this unfair to women, but it's also disadvantageous to men. It's time for men to step up and do their share of support work. On top of counteracting gender bias in the workforce, it will also give men a better understanding of what is going on within the business and what needs to be done to make things run more effectively," Branson wrote in his corporate blog. And when Branson gathered with thirty chief executives for a dinner to discuss how companies can close the gender gap, it was Branson who took notes for the group. Sheryl Sandberg, former Facebook exec and author of *Lean In*, made note of Branson's contribution in her own article on the topic.

If you're the witness . . .

First, make the effort to be a witness. How is office housework handled in your office? If it's not landing in your lap, you may not have noticed the pattern. Look around in meetings. Look around when it's Bagel Tuesday. Notice who is sending out invites. Who is securing the conference room? Do these chores fall to women more often than men? Or to women of color more often than white women? Pay attention as to how the chores are distributed and if it's not being done fairly, jump in. Volunteer to do the chore yourself. Volunteer to create a rotation so that the chores are spread around. Acknowledge the situation and make the fix one of your office chores.

Second, give voice to the pattern. You may be surprised that the issue has gone unnoticed. Says Katie: "A female friend told me a story about a senior staff meeting in which this topic came up. In the meeting, the president asked his new deputy—a woman—to take notes. My friend spoke up and said: 'It's not because she's a woman; the previous deputy was a guy and he took the notes, too.' That comment sparked controversy. The men were shocked that women would even think that was the reason she was taking notes. Just an interesting point on how unaware men can be to the things that make women so angry."

CHAPTER 5

Wow, How Far Along Are You?

How to manage outrageous behavior when you're pregnant at work

Do we really need a chapter about pregnancy? After all, women make up half the workforce, 85 percent of women will become pregnant during their working years and the Pregnancy Discrimination Act was passed in 1978. Aren't we over this?

Apparently not. While companies can't legally have policies that discriminate against pregnant women, the practice still happens.

The National Partnership for Women and Families studied five years of data from the Equal Employment Opportunity Commission (2011 to 2015) and found 31,000 charges of pregnancy discrimination. About one-third of the charges were filed by women claiming they were fired for being pregnant. Twelve percent said their employers made the terms or conditions of their employment impossible; 7.2 percent reported harassment and 4.8 percent said they were the target of disciplinary action.

And today's female workforce will tell you the pregnancy problem persists. Here's one story from one of the younger women we interviewed:

"I was working at a company that had just been acquired. There were several women who were pregnant. The acquisition sparked a change in maternity benefits, and this was revealed at a company-wide meeting." The women learned, at this public meeting, that their promised six-month maternity leave was now just six weeks. The conversation quickly escalated as one woman in particular, who was due in a matter of weeks, protested the change. "And one of the leaders of the company just turned to the woman and said, 'You're so emotional.' It was a cringe-worthy, jaw-dropping moment. Of *course*, she's emotional. This affects her entire life and career trajectory. I didn't think she was being over-the-top emotional, I thought she was actually standing her ground." The man received no discipline for his remark, our interviewee said. And all of the women in the meeting that day left the company soon after having their babies.

Most women in the workforce recognize that despite laws to the contrary, pregnancy is something that can derail them at work. In a study published by the *Academy of Management Journal*, researchers delved into the ways pregnant women work to preserve their images and status at work. Many, the study found, feared they would no longer be perceived as committed and valuable. More than one-third of the women hid their pregnancies from their employers for as long as possible as a strategic move. Many said once news of their pregnancy was out, the mood around them seemed to shift. While the women felt the same, they could tell that their managers and co-workers had started to view them differently. Many women were startled by the change in their co-workers' attitudes since it was their own intention to remain as committed as always to the work at hand.

To counter the image shift, pregnant women engaged in a range of behaviors, from studiously maintaining a consistent work pace and rejecting offers of accommodation to avoiding taking sick days during pregnancy. Many shaved weeks or months off their planned maternity leave, taking less time than allowed by the company, in order to demonstrate their commitment to their jobs. The women felt they had to prove themselves—even though they had already done so in their pre-pregnancy days. It was as if by getting pregnant they had been moved back to square one in their jobs.

Indeed, many women believe that getting pregnant will unravel all the hard work they have done to convince their bosses and coworkers that they are valuable and reliable. Few companies are contradicting that concern when they communicate with their employees. This resonates for women in ways their employers may not realize.

How a woman is treated on the job during pregnancy can have a lasting impact. Angelique's experience certainly puts that into focus.

"The experience of my first pregnancy at PepsiCo was nearly my breaking point, and also became the reason I stayed for another decade," she says.

> It was a Friday morning. I was four months pregnant and hadn't told anyone yet, and suddenly at work I started bleeding. I called my doctor and she said, "Come in right now." I tried to explain that I had a big presentation coming up. I was due to fly with my boss that Sunday to a really important meeting with some very senior people. She said "Angelique. Stop everything. Come. In. Now." I had to go to my boss, tell him in one breath that I was pregnant, having problems, and needed to abandon him for our impending deliverable. He was a father himself, so I was hopeful that he would have sympathy. Unfortunately, he did not. He was annoyed. "Are you sure you have to go? Are you sure you can't do this work?" I was so flustered, so embarrassed, and I cried all the way into the city to meet my doctor. I missed the big meeting. And my

baby was born healthy later that year. But I couldn't wait to quit—there was no way I was going to return to that role and that manager.

After my maternity leave ended, I told my HR manager that I was going to resign. And here's where the story changed for me. She heard me explain the struggles I was having with a baby that never slept and the long commute/small apartment situation, and she just said, "What do you need?" Those four words were so powerful, made me feel so valued and heard. To this day I credit that HR manager with making my loyalty to PepsiCo go through the roof. I took a part-time, remote role for a few years, through a second baby, and when I returned full time, I was Pepsi-loyal like never before. The goodwill created by PepsiCo standing by me when I needed something different made me want to do my absolute best work. And it gave me the line I *always* use when a teammate comes to me with a life event that changes their ability to deliver on work: "What do you need—I'm here to support you." There is no other acceptable response when asked for help.

Even casual interactions can have an impact. Katie saw it.

"I have never had to deal with a pregnancy in the office, but I distinctly remember a woman on my team who really opened my eyes to how off-putting it could be," Katie says. "She was very clearly pregnant and would come back from the cafeteria with reports of people saying 'Wow! You are HUGE!!!'" Two things were clear, Katie says of that incident. The pregnant employee did not appreciate the comments on her size—and she was not going to soon forget who made them.

And the COVID lockdown did nothing to change attitudes. At one

Zoom meeting, Dawn heard a male participant ask a pregnant female participant to stand up and put her belly at camera level so everyone could see how big she'd become.

What the research and anecdotes tell us is that companies are not creating a culture in which pregnant women can freely function—and that can have an impact on the work. When Katie's team member is back from maternity leave, how is she going to feel about the co-workers who made jokes at her expense? What's more, companies are missing the potential upside of dealing with pregnancy and childbirth in a more supportive way—Angelique gave her whole heart to the company that supported her. While many laws and regulations exist to help companies navigate the topic, there is still culture work to be done around pregnancy and childbirth.

If it's you . . .

Communicate. Or don't.

One of the difficulties presented by a pregnant woman in the work-place is that the very personal issue of pregnancy is brought into a very public space—the office. Women will find they are asked a barrage of questions—ranging from their bodily functions to their post-birth plans. To handle, consider what you actually want to say before you're asked anything. To the individual who asks how far you're dilated or how much weight you've gained, you might prepare with some stock answers: "I won't bore you with my medical details," or "I never talk baby biz during work hours," or "Oh, who knows . . . what I'm worried about is how we are going to [launch this product, meet our quarterly numbers, etc.]." Such responses might send the right message.

But don't feel compelled to give a concrete answer to everything. Questions about when you are coming back and how you'll handle your childcare responsibilities are often unknowable. Allow for that gray area.

If you're the boss . . .

Don't shy away from this topic. Creating a culture that is supportive of pregnant women is part of your job.

Lori's take:

> Ask open-ended questions, and let women offer what they need to offer. Don't try to pin women down on every last detail of how they plan to manage their lives once the baby is born. While it's normal to want to know with 100 percent certainty *when* someone will come back and whether they will need/ want any increased flexibility, it's really not feasible for women to fully be able to plan until the baby is born. One piece of advice for companies: think about if you have the ability to hire some sort of professional temps to fill in while someone is out.

At the same time, don't promise what you can't deliver. And that may mean being somewhat comfortable with a vague plan. Says Katie:

> The key thing is to be very supportive. I can recall times where I told the employee she wasn't going to know what she wanted to do until after the baby was born because she would be adamant that she was coming back after x weeks. We often tried to be as flexible with maternity and sick leave too to help find a way to make their paid leave as long as possible. It's very hard as a boss, though, when you have a looming three-month

gap, and you need to figure out how to spread the work around. In small companies, there was no budget to bring in temporary help and in large companies there were rigid policies. I always asked the women to help prepare a list of what we needed to know or do while they were out; my goal was to never have to call them or bother them while they were out. The reality is three months go by pretty quickly in the office so while it looms large at the beginning, the organization usually adapts quite quickly and important things get done.

Take a lesson from Angelique's experience, says Katie. Ask the employee those four words: "What do you need?"

Finally, remember that parenthood doesn't only happen to women. Be sure your discussions and policies include paternity leave, leave granted to adoptive parents or those having children via a surrogate. Research indicates that workplaces routinely fail to support families that are not comprised of a heterosexual couple. A study published by the *Journal of Social Policy*, for example, found that straight parents get more parental leave than male same-sex parents.

If you're the witness . . .

Work on avoiding and dispelling assumptions. If you hear chatter about a colleague who is pregnant that suggests she's now unreliable or uncommitted, call it out. Be a voice for challenging bad assumptions.

At the same time, recognize that well-intentioned assumptions can be equally problematic. Some women told us they were uncomfortable when a man tried to take on some extra work rather than have it fall to her, or when another offered to fetch something in another part of the office so that she wouldn't have to walk the extra steps. While some help may be appreciated, some might be interpreted as a slight. So, the mandate to colleagues is clear: When in doubt, ask. Try: "*What, if anything, can I do to help? Would it be helpful if I took on that extra assignment? Would it be helpful if I ran and got the file folders so you didn't have to make the trip?*" Be fine with whatever answer you get.

And no tummy touching. At all. As they say in preschool, keep your hands on your own body.

CHAPTER 6

I Don't Know How You Do It!

Battling the Superwoman Syndrome

n the novel, *I Don't Know How She Does It*, heroine Kate Reddy lives a frantic, hard-charging existence juggling her job as a senior-level finance executive and her role as a wife and mother of school-age children. In one fraught scene, we find her in her kitchen, late at night, taking a knife to pies she'd picked up at the grocery store. Her goal: make them look homemade rather than store-bought and fool the other parents at the next day's school potluck. As Kate stabs at the crust, she muses on the changing role of women in the world. "Women used to have time to make mince pies and had to fake orgasms. Now we can manage the orgasms, but we have to fake the mince pies. And they call this progress."

Actually, what it's called is "Superwoman Syndrome." This is the internal motivation that pushes women to engage in a constant performance, running full speed to be the best at work and at home. It's applied most often to working mothers, but the stress of the high-wire act applies to all elements of home life. Whether she's thinking about kids or aging parents or dirty laundry or closing on the new house, women are expected to excel in all arenas, professional and domestic. And the most fervent holders of this expectation are women themselves. The Superwoman life is the life we signed up for. We embrace it. Even when it has us up at midnight, distressing store-bought pies to maintain the fiction.

When our bosses and colleagues say "I don't know how you do it," we're meant to internalize that as a compliment—as though we are succeeding at the highest level of womanhood. We're akin to elite athletes or inspired artists, attaining the perfection others can only imagine. I don't know how you do it is high praise.

And also a dangerous myth.

The feeling of doing it all and making it look easy is an alluring experience. Rebecca White, dean of the law school at the University of Georgia, wrote of her experience as a partner-track lawyer with young children. She related one anecdote in which she smugly congratulated herself the day she served as a teacher's helper at her son's preschool in the morning and drove to the state capital to present an oral argument before the court of appeals in the afternoon. She allowed herself what she called the "superwoman" sense of superiority. White burned her candle at both ends to maintain this level of performance, missing long stretches of her son's childhood and enduring the raised eyebrows of female coworkers. "It was never easy, although I did go to great lengths to make it appear so," she wrote.

Let's stop at that final comment. Why? Why was it important to White to be not just successful at home and work, but also to make it *look easy.* When we look hard at that small comment in the otherwise vast sea of women's experience, we see a key problem to be solved: the image issue.

Women engage in a Superwoman Strategy not because it's fun (mostly, it isn't), but because it's the way we've learned to telegraph our commitment to our careers. Any sign of struggle and we fear the workplace will turn on us, Mommy Track us, negate all the years of hard work we've put in.

Is that somewhat paranoid? Honestly, not at all. A woman's valuation of competency can turn on a dime and in ways that do not affect men. In the *Journal of Social Issues*, Amy J. C. Cuddy studied professional women and found working women are sorted into two categories: homemakers—viewed as warm but incompetent—or female professionals—viewed as competent but cold.

Competent or incompetent—which one makes partner?

Cuddy's research was clear. When she looked at men and what

happens to them in the office when they become parents, she saw the reality: men, like women, gain perceived warmth when donning the cloak of domesticity. But unlike women, men maintain their perceived competence.

And in the workplace, perception is a big deal. To that end, women go to great lengths to maintain their competency rating—indeed, to make it look easy. The struggle is well documented when it comes to women trying to be good mothers. But it's hardly the only situation in which the *make it look easy or else* threat looms large.

Katie remembers driving home late one night and crying in the car. "I realized it was too late to call my mom and wish her a happy birthday and I had been too busy to do so all day."

Cie recalls the juggle as on-going:

> Whether it was selling real estate, tending an ailing parent or whatever, my "go to" was to maintain my normal high work output by working really long hours so nothing would slip. I can't think of a time when I had enormous responsibilities outside of work that ever led me to take my foot off the accelerator. Looking back, it seems nuts. I do not think I got any big benefit for this behavior but it took a toll on my personal life, my sleep, and thus my overall productivity.

The behavior not only makes us nuts, it creates an impossible standard for the next generation. Yet in our interviews, they're clearly still chasing it. Here's how one of the rising leaders we interviewed put it:

Superwoman Syndrome definitely exists in our generation as well. My whole life, I have had to be the best at everything I do, and I am the one who expects the most of myself.
I watched my mother expect everything of herself—to be a
full-time, top professional, a mother, a coach, a volunteer. And
I also watched her break down a lot because she never thought
she was good enough. I think that learned experience of never
thinking you are good enough and having to be the best was
something that really stayed with me. I took it overboard when
I was in my twenties also because I wouldn't listen to myself.
If I was sick, I wouldn't stay home, and I would ignore the
symptoms. When I was in a toxic relationship, I got married
anyway. I was so programmed to be Super Woman that I no
longer knew how to acknowledge my weaknesses.

Another perspective from a millennial we interviewed:

This feeling is still real but I believe it's getting better with
every generation. The pandemic fast-tracked everything in a
painful way. You couldn't hide your kids, your anxiety, your
parents' basement, any of it! No woman was living her best
life and it showed. Pulling back "the curtain" helped to show
women just how much grace we can give ourselves. You don't
have to look perfect, you can wear leggings and a blazer, every
meal doesn't have to be fresh, you aren't responsible for every
team-bonding activity. The bar was lowered almost instantly,
and the responsibility for some of those things was *finally*
shared with our partners and male colleagues.

I don't foresee a scenario in my lifetime where women will

fully shake the shackles of the Superwoman Syndrome. Young professional women will realize that while society is understanding, it's only to a point. They are expected to work like men and to manage a home like Mary Poppins. The recent pandemic might have helped us all realize what a joke that is, but unfortunately we're not laughing quite yet!

But what is the option?

Perhaps Superwoman needs a better job description. Doing it all and making it look easy isn't workable.

If it's you . . .

Research is clear: the key to managing work-family balance for women is flexibility from the employer—flexibility to arrange hours, location, and responsibilities to align with family demands. Have an upfront and open conversation with your manager. In a post-COVID world in which Zoom has become a business-as-usual tool, can you lobby for days worked from home? Can you create a flexible work environment that makes the juggle more manageable? The experience of the pandemic may have opened a new window for women in this regard. While previous generations faced skepticism that a work-from-home arrangement could ever be productive, the COVID year suggests that it certainly can be a productive arrangement—if both employee and employer want it to happen.

Also, look for ways the job can flex to meet you. If you find yourself in the Superwoman vortex, consider just how much is really on the line—and just how much feels that way. Take a strategic look at work responsibilities and see what can be managed in such a way that you work smarter rather than harder. Can you shine on a smaller number of projects rather than struggle with a large portfolio? Can you lead a single initiative to success rather than support half a dozen others in their goals?

If you're the boss . . .

Set the right example. Let the team see that you yourself make time for life outside of work, whether it be in the evenings on a regular work week or when it's time for a vacation.

Says Katie:

> I always used to say that work is like a soap opera. Lots of drama every day, but the plot doesn't advance very far in one week. If you try to follow the issues through each day you are on vacation, you will never get a break. If you wait until the end of the week to check in, 95 percent of stuff will be resolved and you can weigh in on the handful of important things that lingered.

When you show you're not "always on," you give the team permission to do the same, she says.

Cie has similar advice:

> As I got older and wiser and tried to actually check out during vacations, I tried to adopt a technique that I learned from one of my best bosses. He would say I am not going to be available while on vacation, however, whatever decisions we (his team) made when he was out, he would respect. He was not going to come back and undo our decisions. He trusted us and was well aware that he was missing a myriad of meetings,

conflicting priorities, and many time constraints so he wasn't going to second guess us. It allowed him to have a good vacation and empowered his team. Win-Win.

If you're the witness . . .

Stop cheerleading the crazy behavior. When you see a woman in high gear, if you're thinking to yourself: *I don't know how she does it!* consider the possibility that the image she's creating is false—and bad for all of us. Instead of marveling at her Superwoman behavior, reach out and see if she needs support. Maybe she doesn't. Maybe she really is Superwoman and it's all going great both at home and at work. But research says that's a mirage and it does women no good at all if we put that Superwoman up on a pedestal and proclaim her to be the ideal.

It just ends up with us in the kitchen, stabbing at the pies, hoping everyone is fooled.

CHAPTER 7

Great Idea, Greg!

How to handle when a guy gets all the credit

A good brainstorming session is often a bit of a free for all. The energy rises and the voices call out and ideas come from all directions. This is where the magic happens. It's exciting. Exhilarating. And often, a pitfall for women.

In a room where everyone is tossing out ideas, everyone seems to hear the men.

Dawn has seen that happen more than once.

> Unfortunately, I personally remember many times in discussions with senior leaders around the table at PepsiCo and again at the NFL, where I had an idea and expressed it. Only to hear minutes later one of my male associates express the same idea—or a slightly different variation of the idea—to rave reviews.

What's more, she recalls, no one seemed to notice this happening. Routinely.

> I genuinely believe those around the table did not realize it was a restatement of my idea. So, what went wrong? Was I too timid or polite in how I suggested it? Perhaps if I had been more animated it would have registered. Was I not strong enough in how I stated the idea? The answers to some may be yes. But unfortunately, there is still some bias to support men.

It's not Dawn's imagination. In a workplace setting such as a brainstorming session, men are heard and acknowledged more often than women. The response can be vivid and unfold right in the moment—such as Dawn suggesting an idea and a few minutes later, a man restating the same concept to rave reviews. ("Great idea, Greg!") Or it can be more subtle. One of the millennial women we interviewed said she spent months trying to get an initiative underway at her company. Then, a new supervisor was added to her team—a man. In addition to being more senior, he had what she called a "captain of the football team swagger." He not only was able to get that initiative rolling almost immediately, everyone in the company was supremely impressed by his vision and ability. And all our female colleague could do was shrug and murmur, "Great idea, boss."

Anecdotes abound, but the science on this topic is important to note. A study published in the *Journal of Applied Psychology* found women are routinely under-credited for ideas and efforts.

The study looked at women and men engaged in the same workplace activity—such as all present in a single meeting or all assigned to the same project team. Women, the study found, are given disproportionately less credit for the success they achieve when they work jointly with men. Lead authors Madeline Heilman of New York University and Michelle C. Haynes of the University of Massachusetts at Lowell used the term "attributional rationalization" to describe the phenomenon. In their study, when a mixed-gender group worked together on a task and it was successful, women were less likely to receive credit for work. Women were regarded more negatively than their male peers. They were viewed as less influential and not having a leadership role.

To many, this conflict calls to mind the *Lean In* solution, posited by Facebook executive Sheryl Sandberg in her book. The Lean In philosophy suggests that women lose out on opportunities in the workplace because they don't dive for the ball—they wait to be recognized rather than adding their voices to the mix and being assertive. They are overshadowed by men because men push forward while women hang back. "So please ask yourself: What would I do if I weren't afraid? And then go do it." Sandberg says.

The problem with that process is that some say it can backfire.

One study, "The Social Consequences of Voice," was published in the *Academy of Management Journal.* Lead author Elizabeth J. McClean of the University of Arizona found that men gain status at the office by speaking up but that women did not get the same bounce from the behavior—and indeed, could receive the exact opposite effect. The study, she said, was designed to address the question of "who gets ahead and why?" of the work world. The results showed "voice" influences social position and that speaking up in a way that focuses on ideas that move the group forward toward an ideal state may be particularly beneficial.

For men.

Women, on the other hand, had a different experience. Women may spend time speaking up, they found, but they don't receive the same benefit as men.

This is a problem for everyone. Clearly, it's a problem for women who fail to get credit for their ideas and efforts. It is more broadly a problem for any organization that hopes to get the best efforts from its employees. If women are not being heard and credited, how many great ideas are simply going unnoticed? How many potential leaders are never getting the boost they need to advance? When women aren't heard, they aren't working to their best potential.

The truth is, the effort to suppress women's voices in the workplace is an ongoing issue. Yoshiro Mori, president of the Tokyo Olympic organizing committee, sparked an outcry when he complained to journalists that meetings with women present take longer than meetings with just men. Women are competitive about securing speaking time, he said. What's more, unless they are given limits, they will talk on and on.

But it's not true that women speak more than men. In a review of the scientific literature on this topic, researchers Deborah James and Janice Drakich looked at 56 studies and found only two said women talked more than men. Meanwhile, 34 of the studies showed the opposite—that men talked more than women.

And the younger women we interviewed said this scenario—this "Great idea, Greg!" moment—is a routine occurrence.

"Have you been listening in on our happy hours?" said one of our interviewees. "It's all we talk about."

Said another: "This has happened to me so many times. I don't know if it's the seniority thing or the female thing. But it's completely obnoxious to me."

Mori was forced to resign over his comments. But the problem persists.

What can you do?

If it's you . . .

Mitzi's approach is to dive in and acknowledge both your input—and Greg's. "For example: Thank you, Greg, for building on my idea. The other thought I had was . . ."

Cie makes a point of getting her ideas out in the open early—before the scrum of the meeting gets more intense. "I found that contributing early got the ball rolling for me and then I was more engaged throughout the conversation. During the meeting I would try to build on my own ideas or as well as the ideas of others and stay very active in the conversation. Sometimes, I'd sprinkle in the reminders of my contribution with 'As I said earlier' and 'I'm glad we agree.'"

Dawn tries humor. "Sometimes I will raise it as a joke: 'Wait a minute—I said the same thing! Do I have spinach in my teeth?'" But it's not her favorite strategy since humor can undermine the intelligence of her original idea. When it's a serious business discussion, you don't want to appear as though you're going for the laugh.

Angelique says this is an issue that requires teamwork to solve—and she borrows from a strategy she learned the women working in President Obama's White House found effective: amplification. When a woman made a key point, other women would repeat it, giving credit to its author. This attaches credit for the point to the woman and makes it harder for a man to claim credit later on in the conversation.

"Female leaders can come together to make sure they have each other's backs," Angelique says. "I've seen this happen effectively in three ways:

1. In the meetings, we actively look for opportunities to call out each other's ideas by name. We use the team chat during virtual meetings to make sure we have each other's backs.

2. After meetings, we actively look for opportunities to reply to group emails where a female colleague should get credit for their great work (and help each other ensure the credit lands!).

3. Before the meetings, we try to look ahead and think: Who is missing from this meeting? (it's often our female colleagues) and we proactively work to get each other included."

Lori has an option that's perfect for the Zoom age: use the chat function to get your idea on the record. "While everyone else is talking over each other, you can thoughtfully comment and use the chat as an extension of a productive discussion." Use it as well to amplify and support the voices of others who may be marginalized. Mitzi agrees, so long as the chat is used in addition to speaking up—not instead of. And one young leader we interviewed added her own spin to the use of the Zoom chat function: Use confident language. Avoid comments such "I just wanted to add . . ." because that type of language can sap your power.

If you're the boss . . .

Pay attention. The research suggests that men—and perhaps even women—tend to miss this imbalance of voice. If you're in charge, how hard are you listening to the voices? Are you noticing the gender breakdown?

President Obama did. When he became aware of the amplification strategy taking place in his meetings, he began to make a concerted effort to call on women and junior aides during discussions.

If you're the witness . . .

Amplification is a strategy anyone can use. Dawn was on the receiving end of this strategy when she was new on a board and an ally amplified her contribution by saying: "I'd like to build on what Dawn said earlier." Whether you are male or female, notice who speaks up, notice whose voice is rising, and use your own voice to note and codify that contribution. Even an ally can notice when someone is trying unsuccessfully to break into a discussion and proactively halt the conversation so that that person can get a word in. Do that by saying, "I think Susan wanted to say something." Your participation can help to steer the conversation—and even your company, in a more inclusive way.

When You Say . . .

Sometimes, it's the things women say that reinforce the stereotypes and make it harder for all women to advance. A lifetime of language is hard to unlearn. We come to our careers with the phrases and constructs and tones we've been using all our lives. In this section, we address the ways women can talk so the workplace will listen.

CHAPTER 8

I'm Sorry for Apologizing

Should women avoid the word "sorry" at work?

S orry this chapter is a bit long.
We just wanted to research some additional details.
We're not experts but we think this adds value.

After reading the above statements, how eager are you to keep reading this chapter? How convinced are you that this chapter will be valuable? How comfortable are you seeing us in a leadership role?

Let's try again.

T hanks for waiting, the chapter is ready for your read. You'll find substantial detail on the topic. We're confident you'll find it a valuable addition to this important conversation.

Notice the difference?

This chapter is about the use of qualifying language—examples include "sorry" "just" and "I think"—and how they impact women in the workplace. It's a topic we are mindful of raising since we're not about blaming women—or how they speak—for the bias they encounter. We don't bring bias on ourselves by our speech any more than we bring sexual harassment on ourselves by the way we dress. The bad actors are responsible for their bad actions.

That said, language has an impact. If you think about how many words you use in a day and how those words swirl around you to create a persona, you can imagine that words themselves are part of your brand. How you use them can sway how others perceive you—whether that's fair or not. If you wouldn't wear a crop top to the office because it would be counter-productive to your professional brand, what words should you leave at home because they don't help you craft a powerful image? Do some words hold us back like a ball and chain? There's plenty of scholarship and popular media discussion on the issue. The issue of women and apology is a hot topic.

Do women over-apologize? Women think they do. Psychiatrist Aaron Lazare, author of the book *On Apology*, reveals that he often opens his remarks to audiences with this question: Who apologizes more? Men or women? Invariably, the women in the audience wave their hands and chorus, "Women!" in reply. The men, Lazare reports, do nothing. The gender split is visible.

And certainly, we saw it. In our role as managers, we observed women apologizing more than men. The word "sorry" was a routine element of their communication—and it affected the way we perceived them. Here's Dawn's take:

> When I was president of Pepsi-Cola North America, I found myself with an equal number of men and women reporting to me. Across the board they were an impressive group. However, I noticed a few differences. One of them was how they handled mistakes. I believe that everyone tries hard and has to have permission to fail occasionally or they will not push themselves.

Well, everything in business never runs smoothly or always well. With the best of intentions, things happen. Mistakes can happen.

But I noted that more often the women would come to me and describe a situation and apologize. And sometimes apologize again. But the men would come in and explain what had happened and more often not apologize but offer solutions to the issue.

This was far more important to me than where or how the problem happened. How do we correct it and do we learn from this to prevent similar occurrences in the future? Apologize to your spouse for coming home later than planned and being late to dinner. You don't need to apologize in the workplace for normal business challenges. Offer solutions and learnings and look strong.

Good advice, but not easy to execute, Angelique points out.

The apology syndrome is a very tricky one to get out of your vocabulary. I find it often comes up when a woman is challenging a colleague, as she finds herself in that no-win situation where women try to be both likable and competent. She'll say, "I'm sorry, I don't understand . . ." when she is trying to clarify something poorly explained by the other.

And when we looked closely, some of us were horrified to find qualifying language all over our own communications. Lori did a review of her email.

A sincere apology when you have wronged somebody is powerful. Learning to say "I'm sorry" in a thoughtful way is a powerful skill and should be practiced. That said, women incessantly apologizing for things is not helpful and can diminish your stature/presence. I'm a chronic apologist. If I told you how many times I said "just" or "sorry" in emails, you would faint. This is something that takes practice for me, but I keep a list of ways to convey the thought without always apologizing.

To be sure, apologizing for an actual offense—such as owning up to an error or misjudgment—is not weakness at all. In fact, it is a sign of leadership to acknowledge and own mistakes. People who never apologize—even in the face of clear wrongdoing—hurt themselves and those around them. It's excessive apologizing that creates a problem.

We've come to realize that while we all hope we will be judged on our work, our words play a role in defining us. We see it as managers, and we know it reflects on our own work as well. What's more, in the digital age, we come to recognize that more of our words are archived for ongoing inspection. Spoken words may be forgotten but digital words are forever and the more qualifying language you use the more impact they have on your body of work. And it does have an impact. "Keep the 'sorry' for real mistakes and always include remedies," says Dawn. "Overly apologetic sounds weak."

But it's a hard habit to shake. When we quizzed our younger generation on this topic, they knew exactly what we were talking about.

I like to try and make a concerted effort not to always say I'm sorry, because someone's told me that once before—you don't need to be like that, you shouldn't say that. But I think that women feel the need to take responsibility even if it's: "I'm so sorry, I can't make this meeting." You don't have to say it like that, but I think women feel like that's being polite—taking responsibility.

Another told us she apologizes all the time—and knows it's a problem for her—so she scans all her emails before sending to edit out any examples of "just" or "sorry."

Indeed, there's an app for that. Tami Reiss, an innovation and product strategist, launched Just Not Sorry as a fix for the qualifying language issue—at least in email. The Gmail plug-in helps you send more confident emails by warning you when you use words which undermine your message. "When someone uses one of these qualifiers, it minimizes other's confidence in their ideas. Whether you're persuading an investor to provide funding, announcing a change in direction to your colleagues, or promoting your services to a client, you are building their confidence in you," Reiss wrote in her launch of the product. "Qualifiers hint to the reader that you don't have faith in what you're saying. The last thing you need is to seem unsure of yourself. We want to make it easy to kick the habit by making it obvious when these qualifiers are holding us back."

It's a great idea and easy to use. But research suggests that the issue of women apologizing is more than a word-choice problem. A study led by Karina Schumann at the University of Waterloo took a deeper dive into the topic to reveal the underpinnings of the sorry issue. She designed a study that asked a group of men and women to keep a diary of how often they apologized. Her research revealed an interesting data point: men and women actually apologize at the same rate *when they think they've created offense.* The difference is, women are far more likely than men to think they've committed an offense. Men, she posited, have a higher threshold for what an offense actually is.

The gender split emerged when it came to calculating offense, she said. "Women are more likely than men to judge offenses as meriting an apology."

In other words, all those Pepsi employees traipsing into Dawn's office weren't demonstrating a gender difference in language choice. The differences they were displaying were more profound. The women felt they had something to apologize for. The men didn't.

And there's no app for that.

What to do?

If it's you . . .

Whether you use an app or simply concentrate on your word choices, be on the lookout for ways to communicate with confidence rather than apology.

"I keep a list of hacks I've borrowed from others to convey the thought without always apologizing," says Lori.

- Instead of "sorry I'm late," practice saying, "Thank you for waiting" (you are still acknowledging you are late, but you are showing gratitude . . . and can move more quickly to start the meeting)
- Instead of saying/writing, "Sorry I didn't realize," say "thanks for pointing that out"
- Instead of "sorry I messed up," say, "Thanks; I'll fix that now"
- Instead of "sorry to bother you," just say "Do you have a minute?"

- Instead of "sorry I didn't understand ABC," go right into "Can you help me to understand ABC?"
- Instead of "so sorry for not responding to your email sooner," say, "I'm responding to your email from May 5 regarding staffing of the new warehouse"

In each case, you'll notice the points get across, but without diminishing your power/influence/stature. Always think about what you're trying to achieve and what you're trying to portray as a leader.

And here's one you can use if you find yourself in a conflict. Instead of sorry, try: "Oh, I remember it differently. Let's solve it and move forward."

When it comes to email, Lori suggests a short pause before typing. "One woman I interviewed said she channels her inner 'Chuck' and she thinks about how a guy would write the email. She says just putting that persona on keeps her from wanting to apologize and use qualifying language. She has found that using the 'what would Chuck do' lens has helped her a lot."

Dawn also looks for ways to address concerns without using the "S" word.

"Part of not having to apologize is also to be clear about competing priorities," she says. "When I am asked to do something that is unrealistic timewise, I say I will try my best and not give personal excuses, but say that there are XYZ other priorities. I will ask if I can have two more days. Is that acceptable? Secondly, if something did not get done correctly in my group, I will say I will look into that and then get back to everyone with status. Avoid the *sorry* word."

And think about why that word may be cropping up in your

conversations. Mitzi notes that sorry may not always mean sorry. "In some ways, 'sorry' is the first cousin to 'um' and 'ah' and is used as a space filler. If you're saying sorry often, it may be a verbal habit you can correct with attention. We can breathe, pause, and say what we need to say without mentioning the word 'sorry.'"

If you're the boss . . .

Coach women to be aware of apologies. It may take some effort but it's an achievable goal.

Says Cie:

> I once had an employee who said "like" all the time— but she refused to recognize that this was an often-repeated, unnecessary word. So, I suggested that we both keep track (a simple check mark on a notepad) and see how many times she used the word "like" in a day. Not surprisingly, initially she was not great at catching herself saying "like," but, as time went on, she became acutely aware and basically eliminated it from her vocabulary. Since this was such a successful technique, I tried it with another employee whose default was to apologize for any and all things. It worked. Putting a spotlight on the issue and having the individual self-grade made a real impact and modified the behavior.

Also, model non-apology language. "I actively worked to replace the language with something more matter of fact," says Angelique. "My favorite is 'let me play that back to you.' It's my way of putting something in my own words to make it more clear to me, and possibly to others. I am literally checking for understanding, but it is not couched in anything missing on my end. I do use it quite often, as I've been told it's my signature phrase."

Katie suggests, "Make sure that you are creating a workplace culture where some risk-taking is not only welcome but encouraged. In that type of culture, if you are not failing on occasion, you are probably not pushing hard enough."

Be sure you're accounting for cultural differences. In some parts of the world, apologetic language is more commonly woven into everyday speech. The "sorrys" you hear may not always need your attention.

And if you're coaching women to apologize less often, be certain that you're giving that advice to men, as well. One of our younger interviewees told us that sometimes, the "stop apologizing" advice may be well-meaning, but misplaced. She told us about a man in her office who has all the same apologizing habits as women. "Yet no one mentions it or comments on it to him."

If you're the witness . . .

Try a modified version of the amplification strategy discussed in the "Great Idea, Greg" chapter. When you hear qualifying language, repeat the phrase without it. When a female colleague uses qualifying language, restate the comment, giving full attribution but with non-apology language.

If you see a female colleague over-apologizing, be a good ally. Take her aside and tell her she has nothing to be sorry for. She may not be aware of the verbal tic. Or she may gain confidence from your expression of support.

And finally, if you hear a lot of "sorry," think broadly about what that means—not just for the individual speaking but for the larger workplace environment. Says Mitzi: "On the surface, this conversation is about saying 'sorry' when you may or may not need to. Below the surface, at a deeper level, there are other things to be considered—like the real or perceived consequences of making mistakes, or the 'air cover' one has to learn from their mistakes, or the environment for taking risks. If our work environments are more inclusive, would the need to apologize be so prevalent? In some ways, 'I'm sorry' is a defense mechanism."

CHAPTER 9

OMG! Talk about Uptalk

Dealing with vocal tone and workplace norms

Let's talk about uptalk.

What is it? It's that little lilt that takes the end of a sentence a half step higher. It manifests when a sentence is ended with a rising pitch intonation, which can sound like the speaker is asking a question.

In some parts of the world—England, for example—uptalk is common among men and women.

But in others, it's become a point of criticism leveled at women. U.S. Senator Kirsten Gillibrand, for example, has voiced her concern that traditionally feminine speech patterns do not allow a female speaker to be taken seriously. "To meet those standards," she says, "you have to speak less like a young girl and more like a young, aspiring professional . . . it's a choice every young woman is going to have to make about how she wants to be and how she wants to be received."

Uptalk has garnered significant attention in the workplace—and on college campuses—as a communication style with issues.

Christopher Peterson, a professor of psychology at the University of Michigan, penned a blog post at the end of one teaching semester called "Upspeak Makes Me Cringe." It recounted his difficulty enduring the trend during a series of student presentations.

Leadership consultant John Baldoni took the issue a step further in his article for *Forbes* "Will Upspeak Hurt Your Career?" In it, he advised uptalkers to seek the help of a voice coach or speech therapist to reduce its usage. "For young women climbing the career ladder, how you sound will influence—rightly or wrongly—how you are perceived. (And the same applies to men)," he wrote.

Except it doesn't—at least not in the same context. Uptalk is a criticism leveled primarily at women.

Traditional advice to women has been to curb the vocal tone in order to, well, be less cringeworthy.

The question we face now is this: Is curbing uptalk good advice? Or is it criticizing women for not sounding more like men?

Historian Yana Skorobogatov writing in the UC Berkeley publication *Matrix* argues that upspeak may have been unfairly associated with a lack of confidence. "Upspeak's defenders argue that the connection between rising intonation and a lack of confidence is socially constructed, a traditional, even outdated linguistic norm, produced and policed by men in order to deprive women of legitimacy." In fact, she writes, research suggests uptalking isn't an impediment to success at all. A study of Texas sororities found senior leaders of the organizations were more likely than junior members to engage in upspeak. A study of Hong Kong business meetings found uptalk more common among meeting chairs than subordinates.

Indeed, we have evolved in our thinking about upspeak—and we place it now not as a vocal tic, but as an example of the ways women are policed in the workplace around elements such as tone, appearance, and wardrobe. We have avoided upspeak in our own careers and counseled other women to do the same. But we wonder now if we have been conditioned to believe that everyone needs to talk like a white man to be taken seriously. To move forward, we need to accept different ways of speaking—and that includes accents and uptalk. We need to do the same around issues of grooming and wardrobe. Says Katie:

> We can still have professional standards, but they can have a much wider tolerance than they do now. We all need to say to ourselves and the women we counsel: What do you want to be known for? After all, the more you push the boundaries of a culture, the more you risk that boundary pushing becomes what you are known for. That said, when I had the audacity not to wear stockings to work, the older ladies in the office all commented. And we need the younger generations in the office to push the boundaries or we'd all still be wearing heels and hose.

Lori suggests applying a filter to issues such as uptalk: What impact does the way she talks have on the business? Thinking about speech in terms of impact—rather than preference—helps to keep the critic focused on the business. People are more than their vocal presentation. "A person is a full person. We should think about how they show up—not just verbally or visually but what their overall work product is like."

If it's you . . .

Apply Katie's advice: consider how you are being perceived and decide if that's how you want to show up. Is vocal presentation a battle you want to fight? Or is it a place where you would prefer to fit in? Understand the impact of your decision either way.

If you're the boss . . .

Embrace the evolution. Just as hose and heels are no longer required, perhaps so too are white male ideas around vocal tone.

Communicate to those you mentor how their speech may be perceived. But make room in your own mind for the possibility that times change and diversity in speech may well be a plus in your organization.

If you're the witness . . .

Consider how you react to vocal tone—are you making judgments based on something like uptalk? Do your judgments match the individual's work product? Unconscious bias is a topic that is often discussed in terms of race and gender. But it can also be applied to vocal tone, accent and other communication styles. Examine your own beliefs and how they play out in the workplace around you.

CHAPTER 10

Is That Okay with Everyone?

Navigating the Likability Maze

On the night she won her second Academy Award, actress Sally Field stood before her peers to accept her Oscar and her exclamation made headlines:

"You like me! You really like me!"

At least that was the sentiment. The actual quote from Sally Field is this:

"I haven't had an orthodox career, and I've wanted more than anything to have your respect," she said. "This time I feel it. And I can't deny the fact that you like me. Right now, you like me!"

It got a laugh—and what passed for meme status in 1985—because it was so true. Who was more likable than Sally Field? She was the face of Gidget, The Flying Nun, Norma Rae, Steel Magnolias. Likable was practically her middle name.

And yet, in the speech before a glamorous and powerful audience of her peers, that's what she said. She was pleased and proud to win—and underscore the knowledge that she was liked.

Women have a complex relationship with likability. Many of us were raised to value it as a personal trait. We were socialized as girls to be nice, to be friendly, to create relationships with others through bonds of mutual affection. We worked hard to be likable. It was instilled in us as a critical element to success.

As we entered the workforce, pleasing others continued to run as a current through our experience. It was not good enough to be good at your job. You also had to work to ensure you were liked—by your boss, by your peers, by everyone around you. If you weren't making others happy, you could never hope to advance. Likability was key to achieving professional goals.

Is likability like nylons—a thing we used to think we needed to exist in the workplace?

Is it a holdover from a time when women were to be sugar and spice and everything nice?

Modern thinking encourages women to see likability as a state of mind—one that can be changed. Alicia Menendez, author of *The Likeability Trap*, encourages women to take control of their people-pleasing instincts. The subtitle of the book is: "How to break free and succeed as you are." Her advice to women is to care less about attaining likability. Focus on self-awareness, she argues. Seek to make your vision seen and understood rather than worrying about who likes you. Consider how much it costs you to be liked and whether that's a benefit to you. Focus on connection rather than approval.

All good ideas. But how much of the likability trap is controlled by women? Self-awareness may not get us out of this one.

Research suggests likability still has an impact in the workplace—for women. For men, it doesn't seem to matter. Leonie Gerhards of the University of Hamburg conducted a study on men and women and how likability played into success. An economist, Gerhards focused on work teams and how they functioned given differing gender make ups. Her results: likability is a key factor for success—but only when one of the team members is a woman. When men are on single-sex teams, she found, it didn't really matter if they liked one another or not. They were able to cooperate and coordinate among themselves. In a mixed-gender team, on the other hand, whether or not participants liked one another became an issue.

"Our results hint at the existence of a likability factor that offers a novel perspective on gender differences in labor market outcomes," she writes. "Basically, what the likeability factor says is that for women, likability is an asset (or equivalently, dislikability is a hurdle) in every one of their interactions. For men, on the other hand, likability matters only if they interact with the opposite sex."

In other words, women always face the hurdle of likability while men do not.

Women who challenge men for top leadership roles find their likability factor becomes an issue. Hilary Clinton certainly had that experience in her primary race with Barack Obama and her presidential bid against Donald Trump. In debates with Obama, she addressed the topic herself and drew out Obama's response, "You're likable enough." In the presidential race eight years later, Donald Trump called her nasty.

Successful women are often criticized for not being nice enough. Anna Wintour of *Vogue* found herself the inspiration for the villain in the novel and film *The Devil Wears Prada*.

We have seen the impact in our own experiences.

Says Cie:

> As a closeted gay teenager, I was so worried I would be shunned and ostracized by friends, classmates, society, teachers/professors, employers, etc., that my strategy was to

be likable. So, from a young age, I got very good at fitting in and I put a high value on being likable.

That was so ingrained for my survival I carried likability into the workplace—even after society became more welcoming and I was more "out" in the world.

Being well-liked certainly paid dividends throughout my career but I probably put too much emphasis on being likable. The likability trap made my leadership style focused too much on building consensus which at times slowed down my decision-making. I believe I could have been an even more effective leader if I were more comfortable making unpopular decisions more often.

And Katie:

I remember we had to do 360-degree reviews at Pepsi where you would have your boss, peers, and the people who worked directly for you rate you on a whole bunch of factors. My 360s were always very good when I was junior. I recall that as I got more senior, there were a couple of times where it felt like someone was nice in person but then took a shot anonymously in the 360s. My feelings were definitely hurt and I took it personally. It was hard to shake that off.

And Lori:

If you've ever done the StrengthsFinder exercise, I'll tell you that I'm a WOO (win others over). It means I love meeting new people and getting them to like me. While this can be helpful

when meeting new people, it can also make me very suscepti-
ble to falling firmly into the likability trap. I have to push myself
to challenge others in meetings, as I sometimes over-think the
long-term effects of someone thinking ill of me. If you're wired
like I am, you can't walk away from the idea of being liked,
but my hack is to remind myself that I've usually been likable
within five minutes of entering a room; I'm friendly, welcoming, and good at small talk and chitchat. I'm in the lifelong
process of teaching myself when the business conversation has
started, that it's okay to disagree productively, always focusing
on the subject matter, never making it personal.

Our younger counterparts note that this remains an issue today.

I see this dynamic everywhere, both high and low on the
power ladder. Women tend to go big-tent, with a focus on consensus building and a need to have everyone leave the room
in agreement. Men don't. I think part of that is how we view
men who take a more "my way or the highway" approach.
Men are seen as being confident and bold or even visionary
when they do disagree. When women disagree, they tend to
be seen as aggressive, inflexible, or defensive. Having said that,
this is an area where I have some hope. For me the goal isn't to
behave more like a man but to make the corporate world more
of a woman's world. I think that more consensus building, and
more openness to ideas and opinions could have a positive
impact on a company. We need to value that more and brute
competitiveness less.

Addressing this issue is complicated, says Mitzi:

> A challenge for women and women of color is that likeability is often in the eye of the beholder, and the beholder can often have a very narrow view of anyone who isn't familiar. Further, if you can't get over the "likability" hurdle, it will be difficult to reach "I know a great guy" status. And if you don't have "I know a great guy" sponsorship, navigating to your dream job could prove to be more challenging and even impossible. How do you get to "familiar" and then to "I know a great guy" status? People have to get to know you—which means you will likely need to share more. This is what moved me from very limited sharing to more sharing. While "being liked" may feel like a popularity contest, for the purpose of effectively engaging with colleagues and building great working relationships, it's necessary. I believe it's important to be respected and liked.

If it's you . . .

It's not your imagination; women are often asked to be people pleasers at work, more so than men. You're not being overly sensitive or nasty to notice. But likability won't get you promoted. Says Katie:

> When I was CEO at Crane, it was no fun making decisions that you knew people weren't going to like. I always tried to remind myself that the job required me to make those decisions and that it is literally the price you pay for the salary you get. When it was really hard, I would imagine some kick-ass boss lady (usually a fictional character—my favorite was Diane Lockhart from *The Good Wife*) and channel her.

If you're the boss . . .

You have a chance to reverse this trap. The University of Hamburg study lays out the fix for the likability hurdle. It's a *likability neutral work culture*—environments that highlight performance and professional behavior among employees but do not see likeability as a prerequisite for successful cooperation. This flies in the face of some culture experts who advocate team-building exercises, off sites, and social hours as a way to build camaraderie and friendships among team members. Indeed, many of us value the teams we're on based on how much we like the other team members. But as leaders, we can look at the friendship factor and understand its pros and cons. While liking colleagues can be a positive experience, we can recognize that likability may be a cultural underpinning preventing women from advancement.

Lori says when likability comes up, keep the focus on work.

> When someone says, she's not likable, come back with "say more about that." Ask the speaker about how the likability (or lack thereof) shows up at work. What impact does that have on the work? Let's try to focus on her leadership competencies and talk about those instead of talking about whether or not we want to have her for brunch.

If you're the witness . . .

Recognize when the likability factor is being applied to others. Is the new female boss referred to as nasty—or worse? Will men tolerate behavior from other men that they won't abide in female colleagues? Likability is a factor that may sprinkle into water-cooler conversations.

Research suggests that even being aware of the double standard for men and women in the workplace begins to diminish it. Start that process yourself the next time someone complains a woman in the workplace isn't nice.

CHAPTER 11

Humanizing or TMI?

What happens when you share at work?

In the Internet Age, very little is left to the imagination.

You may only see your colleagues during business hours, but finding out what they do outside of work is child's play. In a few clicks, you can determine if the new hire is married, where your co-worker went on vacation, and how much your boss paid for her house. You can divine their political leanings, their favorite movie stars and their cooking skills.

During COVID-19, the barriers fell even further. For a year-plus, we looked into the homes of our co-workers and saw their furniture, their art tastes, their bookshelves. We saw their spouses, children, and pets. Whatever veil we had between work and home was pulled back and everything we were at home was on display via Zoom. It was a time when you could learn that your teammate had a green thumb, your client was house-training a new puppy, and your supervisor was a Red Sox fan.

We also knew whose new baby had colic, whose relationship was on the rocks, and who had noisy neighbors.

With all that forced sharing going on it may be a good time to talk about sharing in general—and when it can tip into oversharing.

The line between sharing and oversharing can swing widely on a generational basis. Those raised in an era of landlines may find it off-putting to be quizzed on issues they were schooled to treat as personal, and therefore not to be discussed in a professional environment. But digital natives have an entirely different relationship with personal information. For the younger generations, living a life online is fully appropriate—it's the way you reach out and connect with the world.

And indeed, the rise of technology does more than just facilitate this sharing. Silicon Valley, which brings us the tools of digital sharing, is generally a big proponent of creating personal connections in the workplace. Tech CEOs often place a high premium on work-based friendships, encouraging games, outings, and team-building exercises that encourage participants to share their feelings. These are successful, ground-breaking companies. Their processes are admired and often copied. And their POV is embraced by younger workers. A survey conducted by LinkedIn found 67 percent of millennials are willing to share once-taboo personal details, including salary and family issues, with their co-workers.

Much of the buzz around sharing in personal context is highly positive. Brene Brown, for example, has spent years studying the topics of courage, vulnerability, shame, and empathy. Her TED talk, "The Power of Vulnerability," has been widely viewed. She encourages us to be vulnerable, to share. Even in the office. We wear our heaviest armor at work, she says. We need to be comfortable being uncomfortable.

For life's truly big issues, sharing creates a necessary humanity in the workplace. Says Dawn:

> There are situations when personal information is very important and the timing of when and how to share it is important. I sadly have had the experience of losing a child

about three years ago. Many in my board circle and prior business relationships reached out to express their support. But in person, some felt warm and able to acknowledge my situation in a way that was supportive and not too prying. I remember being on a board call for Nvidia three weeks after she died and the CEO stopping the meeting to say how sad my voice sounded and how much he wished he could help. It made me feel supported without unduly focusing on it and making me feel even sadder. Another board call for a different company never mentioned anything and in fact when I showed up for the first in-person meeting post her death, the CEO did not say anything to me. People are uncomfortable with a sad situation like this. But ignoring it makes it worse and does not make one feel supported at that company.

I would advise co-workers and bosses to acknowledge loss, ask what they can do to support, and remember that loss takes much time and after months have gone by, the pain and need for support is still high. This can apply to any family loss.

Now, when I join a new board where no one knew my history, I face a separate challenge around sharing. When do I tell them? If too many years go by and I do not mention it, am I not bringing my whole self to the company? I do feel that people at the right time appreciate the candor and often one finds someone else who can relate to you in that situation. In the case of a child, it usually comes up when someone innocently asks "how many children do you have?"

Lori faced this decision when she was diagnosed with cancer.

When I was diagnosed with breast cancer in 2008, I had an immediate choice to make—was I going to be private about it (like my mom chose to do when she was diagnosed in 1973) or was I going to be public about it? Maybe because of the bad memories of wondering what my mother's "under arm surgery" was really about or maybe just knowing that being public was a way to help others, I decided to share my story each step of the journey. I had just started a new role working for the president of Pepsi North America. I met with him on Friday morning to talk about my new role, and eight hours later, I received the bad news about my diagnosis. I remember calling his admin early the following week to ask for *another* meeting with him, this time to share my news. Without skipping a beat, he asked what support I needed from the company and how he could be helpful. He told me that I should transition into the new job at any pace that made me comfortable, and then finally, he said, "I know you'll fight cancer with the same energy you've been fighting the cola wars for the past two decades." It was such a simple meeting, but it meant so much to me. I worked throughout the next eighteen months, taking time when needed for my six surgeries and five months of chemo. I felt energized (dare I say "normal"?!) when I went to the office, and not surprisingly, I did great work, because I wanted to . . . not because I felt any pressure. So, the first part of the story is, by my sharing, I allowed my boss, and the company writ large, to support me.

The second part of the story is that by deciding to share my story, I was able to help others. I told everyone what was happening and even allowed the company to feature me on a Gatorade bottle that raised money for a breast cancer charity. Now *that* is public—having a picture of you (with barely any hair after finishing a course of treatment!) on grocery shelves throughout the United States! Importantly, I cannot count how many times over the past twelve years, Pepsi colleagues have reached out and asked if I would talk to a wife/sister/ mother who had recently been diagnosed. In short, by telling my story, I allowed the company to show me its kindness, and I was able to use my not-so-fun experience to help others.

In fact, the research is pretty mixed on sharing details of one's personal life at work. There are some who prefer to keep home life as more of a mystery. But there's a flip side that warns us to be wary of *under-sharing.*

Harvard professor Leslie John studied personal information and how we judge those who share—and those who do not. She and her team designed an experiment to uncover how we react when we hear personal details, especially those that may reflect negatively on the sharer. In the experiment, John uncovered a surprising result: those who did not disclose personal information were viewed as "hiders" and judged unfavorably. Participants were more favorable towards those who shared—even if it was information that didn't necessarily make the sharer look good. The "revealers" were viewed as honest, and that made up for whatever negative detail they'd made public. On average, 80 percent of participants favored the revealer over the hider. "I thought this was a false positive at first, but we replicated it many, many times," John said in an interview with the *Harvard Business Review*. "I was shocked."

The influence of the Internet may be at the root of this trend, she noted. In an age when many have at least some presence on social media, a reticence to share personal details may be viewed as unusual, and even suspicious. Disclosure, she said, is becoming the norm and therefore non-disclosure is anomalous. Those intent on maintaining privacy may risk what she calls "undersharing." They don't perceive the trust issue at play.

That said, not everyone is built for sharing. Says Mitzi:

> I'm sure I fall in the camp of "under sharing" which is an improvement from not sharing. I remember hearing mentors talk about their "weekday" car and their "Sunday" car. This was a reference to keeping their personal and professional lives separate and a belief that doing so was beneficial. Eventually, I found it difficult to build meaningful, collaborative relationships at work, without sharing more about me—personally.

Research suggests there is a line between sharing enough to gain trust and oversharing to the point of professional damage. That line, says Babson College professor Kerry Roberts Gibson, is the one drawn between worker and management.

Her study of self-disclosure in the workplace found that sharing personal details with a peer is fine—but bosses should be more guarded when sharing with subordinates.

Gibson's research looked closely at the sharing of personal details in a task-related context. Her study created mini-competitions for her participants that were designed to mimic workplace activities such as working on a team. What she learned: no matter how much everyone likes to hear a bit of gossip, no one wants to hear the boss's weaknesses. As juicy as it may be, knowledge of the weakness interferes with the work. In this context, disclosure can chip away at the leader's status.

In other words, it's fine if your co-worker is going through a messy divorce. But if it's the boss, then your perception of the boss's ability may sink. The boss's weakness may undermine the work. And when you're considering that topic, remember that if you get promoted, today's peers are tomorrow's direct reports. Says Cie: "I would recommend really thinking through what you feel comfortable sharing with your work friends—keeping in mind you do not want to undermine your authority if you become the boss."

We found the millennial and Gen Z women we interviewed also faced this issue. "I'm aware that boundaries are hard in general for women, because we're socialized to put others' needs before our own," said one.

How to handle sharing, oversharing, undersharing and the ripple effects of all?

If it's you . . .

Read the room. Workplaces all have their own cultural rules around sharing. Listen to what others are doing before you make your own decisions about how much or how little to share. You may agree with the culture as you find it—or you may decide you want to buck the norm. But know the water temperature before you dive in.

Recognize that your listener may not be totally enjoying the sharing. Says Cie:

Most of us operate our lives in the middle of the excitement range between 40 and 60. I had a very talented employee who lived her life between 0 and 20 and 80 and 100. She had huge highs and huge lows and always drama, drama, drama in her personal life. Every Monday morning, I would hear all about the weekend's adventures which often featured lots of partying, fights with her significant other, locks being changed, and the occasional police report. Sometimes listening to that level of chaos would make my back sweat. And, knowing the chaos, it would sometimes influence the assignments I would send her way. Even though she was very capable, if I had a time-sensitive project, I was sometimes hesitant to pull her in as I knew too much and felt she would be distracted.

Mitzi recommends figuring out what you want to share about you, so people get to know you as a person and not just as an employee. Show you care about colleagues as individuals. Share and engage to build solid working relationships.

If you're the boss . . .

Be mindful that your team looks to you for leadership. While you may not want to be inscrutable, sharing all your woes may leave them wondering if you're up to the job. Share enough to humanize you. Find a middle ground.

If you're the witness . . .

For the big issues, show your human side. Says Lori:

We all struggle with what to say when someone has a personal tragedy. As someone who received so much love from my Pepsi family, my community, my customers, and my friends (when I had a personal health crisis), I will tell you that any expression of kindness is appreciated. An email, a text, a voicemail, a card, anything. I wasn't judging. I just felt compassion. No one treated me like I was a victim who was going to die; everyone just sent good thoughts, hugs (in an appropriate way!), and kindness. I was appreciative of any good thoughts whether it came from a very good friend/colleague or someone who I knew less well from a project team. It was all helpful. So, if you're ever worried that you're not a close enough colleague to send a note, don't worry. Everything is appreciated.

But for the smaller ones, your obligations are different. If an oversharer is monopolizing your sympathetic ear, you can try to redirect the conversation. Or, if that doesn't work, it's okay to say, "Maybe we could talk about this another time." Whether you're sharing or not, your feelings matter.

Section Three

What's Unsaid . . .

There are hurdles that rise up when nothing's been said at all. How can women spot the obstacles nobody ever discusses? How can we handle the roadblock when we see it but nobody else speaks up? What's unsaid looms large in our work lives. In this section, we name and address the invisible walls.

CHAPTER 12

At the Table But Not in the Conversation

Tips for breaking in and being heard

Much of corporate America runs on relationships, trust, and familiarity. Often those relationships can bloom from shared experiences and shared conversations in the workplace. So, what do you do when your boss spends the first fifteen minutes of his Monday morning staff meeting talking with two male colleagues about the ins and outs of the weekend's football games? You can feel that they are bonding while you are sitting quietly at the table waiting to talk about action plans to drive sales this quarter, but you're not sure how to jump in.

This is a common scenario. It's a subtle, but routine problem women encounter in the workplace—and one that managers and allies may miss. By all appearances, you're in: you have the job, you have a physical seat at the table, and ostensibly, you can jump in and join the conversation any time.

But that's easier said than done.

Breaking into a conversation in progress takes guts in any setting, but in the pre-meeting chatter, it's a gauntlet. Suppose you get into the conversation and make a mistake since the topic is not one you know well? Suppose you say something that offends? Or worst of all, suppose you try to get into the conversation and they ignore you?

Plenty of women will simply sit out the fifteen minutes in silence checking email on their phones rather than risk stepping on a career landmine.

The problem with that strategy is that you essentially opt out of the career accelerant that is bonding.

We have been there.

Angelique lived it during football season. "The weekly executive staff meetings used to be dominated not only by sports, but specifically by the Eagles, as several of the men on the team (including the CEO) were fans," she says. "By the time the meeting was scheduled to start, there was already deep banter that was hard to break into, especially if you were not an Eagles fan."

The experience can expand well beyond sports. One of the millennial women we interviewed found herself on a team with a group of men who were all from Dallas. She wasn't. Meetings were often preceded by fifteen minutes of discussion of the city of Dallas, the state of Texas, and other related regionalisms. "If it were two women talking, I would have interjected: 'Oh, tell me more about that. That's interesting.' But with men, I felt this does not sound like a conversation they want me to be in." And so, her team meetings always started with fifteen minutes of silence while she waited for small talk to end and the meeting to begin.

When we began researching this book, we discovered there were some work situations that challenged us as women on a daily basis—but when we mentioned them to the men in our lives, they were truly surprised. There are hurdles in the workplace that women face and men often do not see. The "at the table but not in the conversation" scenario is one of them. This is a hurdle for women that men often set up by accident—at least much of the time. While there are certainly bad actors out there, we're willing to bet that neither the Eagles' fans in Angelique's past nor the Dallas natives that worked with our millennial colleague had any idea the pre-meeting chitchat was in any way problematic.

Research suggests a reason for this misunderstanding. In academic studies of gender and conversation, science reveals that men engage in the same conversation patterns no matter who they're talking to. Women, on the other hand, shift to adapt to men.

In her popular book, *You Just Don't Understand: Women and Men in Conversation*, Deborah Tannen discusses a workplace study conducted in a unique way: via eavesdropping. A researcher spent time in the corporate dining room of a bank—one that the bank officers used for lunch. The study found that men, when sitting with only other men, talked mostly about business. Secondary topics included food, sports, and recreation. Women, when seated only with other women, talked about people—friends, children, partners, and other personal relationships. Secondary topics for the women included business and health—especially weight control.

When men and women sat together, they naturally compromised. Neither group got its first choice of conversation topic. Instead, the group gravitated to topics popular across genders. But in these mixed-gender groups, women still flexed to meet the men. When they talked about food, the group followed the male conversation pattern by focusing on foods and restaurants rather than weight loss or health. When they talked about recreation, the group emphasized sports and vacations over personal exercise. Both genders compromised on topic. Women took the extra step of compromising on conversation style.

When we were coming up in our careers, we worked hard to succeed at the men's conversation rules. We could see the upside.

Mitzi was always a sports fan—and that paid off for her.

As a former college athlete, the Monday morning conversations that revolved around sports were music to my ears. I could quote facts, stats, plays, and names as well as most of my male colleagues. The conversations about sports provided a way to share experiences around something, outside of work, that mattered to my male colleagues. I looked at each of those moments as opportunities to build camaraderie and put deposits in the "relationship" bank. Engaging in sports conversations put me in a better position to lead the conversation to the topic I wanted, when the sports conversation ended.

Katie didn't come to her career with a love for sports—but she learned.

I figured out pretty early on that sports were the social language of the workplace and if I wanted to be part of it, I needed to start paying more attention. I don't necessarily think it's a bad or good thing that this is the case—it's just a fact. If I were living in a foreign country, I would learn the language and this didn't feel much different to me. And while I couldn't make up for 30-plus years of not paying close attention, I could pretty easily catch up with what was going on right now. In some cases, I found that a well-timed point or anecdote could enhance my credibility. But I also found that once I started paying more attention, it did become more interesting to me. Like any story, once you start following the plot and the characters, it becomes more interesting. You just have to make it through a chapter or two. I might not watch every game or every sport, but it wasn't hard to keep up with what was going on with local teams and/or postseason performances. And while I wouldn't be in the thick of a deep debate about a certain player, for example, I would be interested generally in the discussion and might pick up a good tidbit to use in another conversation. Once my job became more directly sports-related, I did have to study a bit more. I watched SportsCenter every morning while I got ready for work, and I actually would quiz myself on things that many boys master in early elementary school: teams, divisions, conferences.

But as we rose in the management ranks, we began to see the conversation issue in a different way. It was a regular occurrence that excluded some—primarily women—from the casual conversation of the workplace. "As I got more into leadership positions, I tried to make sure I created an inclusive environment in which the majority of folks could participate," Cie said.

Angelique sees the meetings differently now.

Once you are made aware that your colleagues may be experiencing the same meeting or work environment differently from you, the mindful people will be looking for ways they can help. I'd love to inspire people to think about how they can be an ally. Who in the room is not being heard? Who is not at the table but should be? I have deep gratitude to the people who "saw" me and brought me forward, or privately coached me to improve my impact. I'm trying to do the same whenever I can. Lately, I feel most conscious of the voices of color in the room. Are they there? Are they being heard? It's often so unconscious that you could be accused of "overthinking it." But we must overthink this in order to make any real progress!

If it's you . . .

Learning the language is a good option—it's worked for many. But there are also tweaks you can make to ensure your engagement in the casual chitchat goes well.

Lori advocates for what she calls "the invisible pivot." Don't worry about what you don't know; pivot the room to a topic you do know. "If you're very graceful about it, people won't even realize it's happening. As people are going on and on about the Sunday games, I would say, 'OMG, did you watch the commercials during the game? I saw that XYZ company introduced a new ad campaign and there was so much controversy on Twitter about whether it was too edgy for that brand. What did you all think about the ads?'"

For what it's worth, she said, the pivot applies well beyond sports. "The same strategy can apply when everyone is talking about the *Game of Thrones* season finale and you don't watch GOT. You might say, 'I didn't watch it but I'm so curious about what you're going to binge watch now that GOT is over. My sister thinks I should watch *Schitt's Creek*, but I'm not sure. Do you have any suggestions? What is your family into?'"

The pivot worked for Dawn during her years as chief marketing officer of the NFL. Dawn is a big football fan. But during the Monday morning quarterback conversations at the NFL offices, Dawn often found herself at the table with former NFL players. "Their knowledge and perspective on calls was at a professional experience level. So, I contributed by adding something my husband or daughter said to try to steer the conversation to a fan perspective where I could hold my own. Or I would ask how people thought the team being discussed would fare the following week. Make the conversation about future possibilities versus facts."

Another Dawn tip: Take the time to get to know the families of your co-workers. No matter how thrilling the sports talk, many people will happily change the subject to themselves and their loved ones.

Cie adds: Whatever you do, make the effort to get into the pre-meeting chatter. Don't just sit there checking your phone. "Getting into flow of the pre-conversation makes it so much easier to actively participate when the real business meeting starts. I found that it took away any awkwardness of trying to find the right time to jump into the flow as I was already in the flow."

If you're the boss . . .

What we all thought was a personal challenge when we were coming up in the ranks, we all see as a new mandate now that we are in senior roles. A seat at the table is a good start. It must be followed by active inclusivity. "The lesson for leaders is to keep focused on the room dynamics. Watch to see if only a few people are participating, and look for ways to make the conversation more inclusive/available/welcoming to others," said Lori. Actively invite others into the conversation.

Says Mitzi: "As a leader, another way to promote more inclusivity is to rotate who picks the topic of discussion. Where the need for more diverse and inclusive thinking is greater, a bolder, game-changing way to foster more inclusivity is to bring more diverse talent to the table. Change the people sitting in the chairs; you most likely will change the conversation."

If you're the witness . . .

Take a cue from Angelique and her new perspective on how workplace conversations are perceived. Consider that the way you experience a meeting or other workplace interaction may be different from your colleagues. Are you reaching out to connect with everyone in your work group? Do your conversations include them? Or are you gravitating to people who are like you—and like to talk about the same things you do?

CHAPTER 13

No Invite

When the fun's beginning but you're left out

No, you're not having a high school flashback. In fact, if there's something fun going on and you weren't invited, you may be having just another day at the office. Women are frequently left out of extra-office fun.

The lack of invitation to social events is an under-noticed barrier in the corporate workplace. It's commonplace for gatherings to happen outside of work—drinks at the bar, a sports outing, a run at lunchtime—to which men are invited and women are not. And do women shrug at the lack of invitation? Usually. Maybe they don't think the gathering sounds like all that much fun anyway. Maybe they think they don't have the time to socialize. Maybe it's embarrassing to be left out and they'd prefer not to spotlight the issue. But the absent invitation is real.

We've all seen it.

Cie recalls a convention that took place in Las Vegas. When the day's work was over and the official meetings ended there was a core group of attendees—all men—who would stay up late playing blackjack. Cie likes to gamble and is a good cardplayer.

But none of the men reached out to include her. She took it as a miss rather than an active exclusion. "They were just going with the assumption most women would not be interested in gambling late into the evening," she says.

No invite.

Dawn, too, faced the no-invite scenario.

I served on the board of Lowe's Home Improvement stores for fourteen great years. We met five times a year at their headquarters in Charlotte, North Carolina. Meetings started midday on a Thursday and ended with lunch on Friday.

At the time I was serving on the board of the LPGA and became the chair of the LPGA. Many of the largely all-male Lowe's board (I was the sole woman for twelve years until we added one more woman) loved to talk golf with me. They assumed I had to be pretty good to serve on the LPGA board and a few asked my handicap, which was a thirteen at the time. Not bad for a man or woman. We talked about our favorite courses we liked to play or personal upcoming trips in the downtimes around the meetings.

I found out that varying members would stay Friday afternoons and play golf at a local club. Sometimes with the CEO of Lowes. I hinted that I would love to play one time. But I never got the invitation.

High school, all over again.

Some might argue that the absent invitation does not rise to the level of gender bias. But they're wrong. And it only takes a little thought about the workflow of the average corporation to see the issue. It's true that work takes place in the office—in cubicles and conference rooms and corner offices. But when women are not invited to non-work events, they miss out on the opportunities to bond, network, and engage with colleagues in a relaxed setting. If you've ever seen a movie in which the heroes come up with a great idea and sketch it on the back of a cocktail napkin, you know: non-office gatherings can be the places where the magic happens.

Not being invited to those places puts women at a disadvantage.

When you don't get the invitation, you don't get the chance to kick back with colleagues. You don't get the chance to share stories and build connections. You miss out on the chance to hear idle chatter that may inform work efforts. In short, the work conversation is going on without you.

This is not just about fun and games. Research reveals these extra-curricular activities are key to advancement to senior ranks. A study by workplace scholar Karen Lyness highlights the problem. When she looked into the different ways men and women advance in the workplace, she found the softer elements of human relationships played a big role. When women were asked to discuss their barriers to advancement, they most often cited their "lack of cultural fit" closely followed by "excluded from informal networks." These far outpaced issues such as getting plum assignments. From the women's perspective, the roadblocks were cropping up outside of the everyday work activities.

Some have argued that this is simply a communication problem: women wait for a concrete invitation while men simply add themselves to any group in a casual way. But research doesn't back that benign account. In fact, it suggests men know full well that when they plan outside activities, they are closing gender ranks. A study by Rosabeth Moss Kanter showed the incursion of women into the upper management ranks actually triggered a defensive response. The men, she noted, responded to women in their midst by exaggerating their camaraderie and emphasizing their differences from the women. Still another study by Sally Davies-Netzley noted women in senior management ranks are routinely excluded from informal networks of male peers.

"Informal network" is really just an academic way to say "work friends." We spend so much of our time at work that it's natural we make friends. But the rules that governed the playground and left some kids standing on the sidelines at recess should not be in play when careers are on the line. Women make work friends, just as men do. But men are able to use their work friendships to advance while women often lack this option. And the option starts with the invitation. When the men are going out for lunch or after work or to hit the golf course during a business trip, who do they invite? And who do they leave out? The research answers that.

The invitation issue shines a spotlight on an often overlooked element of gender bias. Invitations are not like salaries or promotions—they're not tracked and analyzed by HR. They're not set as diversity milestones. In fact, many managers would say they're not part of the workplace purview at all. But few will argue that social interactions are part of the fabric of any company. They are part of how we come together as people to merge our talents and do great things. Sometimes that happens in cubes and conference rooms. Sometimes it happens over lunch or cards or raw bar happy hours. We often play close attention to the advancement of women at work by using workplace metrics such as salaries, promotions, responsibilities, and accolades. But are we looking outside of work for places where women face hurdles? Are we identifying ways to battle those barriers, too?

Even when we do see them, do we consider the lack of invitation a true problem? How often do we let the lack of invite slide—*Who wants to go for a run at lunch anyway? Why would I want to hang around in a dive bar after work when I could get home to my family?* The situation is easy to dismiss when there's plenty else that needs doing.

But that mindset only makes it harder for women to get into these casual gatherings and become part of the social fabric of the leadership ranks. When we take ourselves out of the mix, the power structure will not chase after us.

Key to the invitation issue is recognizing that these "after work" activities are actually still work. They may take place in non-work settings, but the networking and bonding will resonate through the workplace. When women do not get the invitation, it's akin to being excluded from the morning meeting. Whether or not it looks like work does not matter; work is happening. Says Mitzi: "We're fooling ourselves if we think off-site conversations don't involve talking about work—if we think it's all about golf, football, or Poker." The informal, off-site discussions are often where big "what-if" ideas are born and discussed, she says.

And worse, the invitation issue can be clouded by other discussions around gender. Angelique was already herself in an executive position when she saw the invitation issue playing out—for others. "One of our C-suite male colleagues was famous for inviting guys he liked to go for a scotch. Those who liked (or pretended to like) scotch had a great opportunity to bond with an influential person on the executive team. But he never invited any women. Some said that showed restraint; he didn't want to appear inappropriate. But others said it was unfair. Women didn't have the chance to build a relationship with that individual."

That's a great example of exclusion dressed up as protection. But no matter how you view it, men were out drinking with the boss. Women were not invited.

We wondered if this invitation issue was still relevant—so we asked our younger colleagues to weigh in.

Turns out, they see it all the time.

Says one:

> It's a regular thing. The guys make their plans while standing around in their cubes. The women were right there, but none of us said anything. They organized after-work drinks,

things like that. If you asked them about it, they said: Oh, it's a guy thing. You probably wouldn't have fun.

And for another, the boss was part of the problem:

> At my old job, there were no rules, no structure, and the men would take two-hour lunches with my boss because they were all friends. I was never invited. I can't imagine the looks I'd get if I took a two-hour lunch. The worst part was knowing the guys were out there, talking about the projects we were all working on, getting all this time with the boss. At my current job, that sort of social exclusion is not allowed. There are rules that social functions must be inclusive.

The invitation issue is loaded with assumptions. The men assume the women won't have any fun at their activities. The women assume the men are excluding them intentionally. Senior managers may assume that anything going on outside the office really isn't any of their concern and doesn't demand their attention. But the invitation issue is one that needs to be called out and addressed by all parties. Women who notice the issue—whether it is an intentional slight or an accidental oversight—need to confront the problem.

How should you handle the absent invitation? You have options.

If it's you . . .

Try the Cie method: invite yourself. Vegas was hardly the only time Cie found herself at a casino location. "Atlantic City, San Juan, or Reno, gambling venues for key meetings with customers or distributors was common. Usually, the most fun and key bonding time happened very late—after the dinner and after the dabblers headed to their rooms." Cie was seldom actually invited, but she made it a point to join the late-night card players. "The guys loved it. They were always pleasantly surprised that I knew the game and was an aggressive gambler. Some of the hilarious stories coming out of those evenings are stories I retell to this day." Cie thinks the men assumed women wouldn't want to gamble with them. "And that assumption was indeed true for most of the women from the company, but it was not true for me. And, of course, the bonding that I experienced in those late evenings laughing in Vegas built trust and relatability that bled into the workplace."

Cie's tips: If the event is informal, invite yourself and bring someone else along. That will reduce any awkward feelings. If it is a formal event, make some inquiries as to how the invitation list was created. You may discover a reasonable explanation as to why you're not on it. Or, your inquiry may be enough to let the organizers know you'd like to be on the list—and generate an invite.

Another option, from Mitzi: Find a colleague who is invited and see if that person can influence on your behalf and get you invited. "Be proactive! Be persistent in figuring out how to get invited—in a way that works for you. But get invited! Consider the 'out of the office networking' part of your job, part of the work you need to do."

Creating your own invite is a powerful move. But that doesn't always do the trick. Dawn made the effort to get herself into the Lowes golf game—she talked golf with them, made clear she was a strong player and would love to join them—and the men never asked. For those in a Dawn situation, reach back to your high school days for another tactic.

Plan your own party. This is Lori's go-to method. "I find one of the best ways to avoid being in an awkward situation is to volunteer early to be the planner," she says. Once holding the planner baton, Lori goes all-in on inclusive activities. She's organized cooking classes, bowling, puzzle tournaments. And when she organizes, she holds the invitation power. Her common theme: all ages, genders, and athletic abilities welcome.

Dawn notes that planning an alternate activity isn't always practical. But there are other ways to rearrange the situation.

> When there was a golf game and I was not invited, it would be weird for me to plan another different activity. Rather, I might have asked others to play who were not included in the foursome and try to create another golf game. Even if only one other was interested, I believe it would have resulted in everyone pivoting to have two groups of three. Bottom line: They may not realize they've caused offense. Help them to fix the situation.

If you're the boss . . .

Don't ignore the social currents around you. The way your reports behave together—whether in or outside the office—has bearing on your success. If yours is a team where men bond and women watch from the sidelines, that news will get around. You have the power to face the "no invite" barrier and quash it.

Make clear that social events are to be inclusive. Give voice to the issue and let it be known that it's not acceptable to exclude.

Then, show everyone how it's done. Organize team lunches and other outside-the-office activities to model inclusive behavior. Send out invitations, get creative (Taco Tuesday, Pizza Friday). Create events that will break up known cliques in the office. Be sure to schedule some during work and some after work hours, that way everyone can participate. Articulate the value of these gatherings to everyone. Pay special attention to extending inclusive behavior to new team members. Make this part of their on-boarding experience. Set the tone for the new team member by creating a sense of belonging from the start.

And don't make assumptions. Says Dawn: "Regarding the Lowes situation, I am sure they thought I had to get back to my family and did not want to make me feel like I had to stay. As the organizer of the event, do not make that assumption. Invite me and I will tell you if I cannot stay."

If you're the witness . . .

Perhaps you're invited, but you can see someone who is not. Don't blow it off as none of your business. Instead, see it as your problem to resolve.

If you're in a work-related social gathering that's not inclusive, call it out. Even if the poker game has always been "just the guys" or you can't imagine the women in the office would like pickup basketball, point out that engaging in non-inclusive behavior is bad for everyone.

Encourage the group to change its ways.

Extend the invitation yourself. Says Mitzi:

Reach out and include your female colleague who is not invited. It's the events that women are not invited to that lessen their ability to become better "work friends." These are the forums for having others get to know us. They are the pathway to achieving the status of Good Cultural Fit.

Make a point of approaching someone who has been excluded and inviting them to the next gathering. Let the invited group members know you're doing it.

CHAPTER 14

Get Paid Like Paul

How men get raises and how you can, too

A post making the rounds on social media offers this advice to expectant parents: at your gender reveal party, forgo pink or blue cupcakes or gender-themed fireworks, and instead, hand out wallets to all your guests and have them inspect the contents at the same time. If it's a boy, the wallet will contain $1. If it's a girl, 79 cents.

It's funny. Sort of.

The wage gap between women and men remains a pernicious reality of the workplace. Across the spectrum of age, industry, and race, women earn less than men. The Center of American Progress collected this data:

For every dollar earned by a white man, this is what women earn:

White women: 79 cents

Black women: 62 cents

Hispanic women: 54 cents

Asian women: 90 cents

American Indian or Alaska Native: 57 cents

That's based on U.S. Census data generated in 2018. In the post-COVID era, in the wake of massive job loss and reduced hours incurred by women, those numbers are likely to look much worse.

Women over the decades have boosted their participation in the workforce. They've elbowed their way into once-male bastions of law, medicine, and finance. They've broken the glass ceiling to run companies, lead armies, and launch into space.

And yet the wage gap persists.

Why does this happen? The Center for American Progress (CAP) offers several reasons. Women still tend to be found in occupations that historically pay less—jobs like home healthcare aides and childcare workers. Women also tend to have fewer years in the workforce, taking time to accommodate caregiving and other unpaid labor. That adds up to differences in years of experience between men and women. Angelique knows that story.

> I'm a case in point: I went down to part-time status when I had my two children for a total of three years before I came back full time. In that time, of course I was not able to progress—and when I returned, I had to rebuild my case for promotion to the next level—which put me at least five years behind others who had demonstrated similar impact, with a compounding effect on my earnings.

But none of these eclipses the primary factor limiting women's pay, CAP says, and that is discrimination.

"Gender-based pay discrimination has been illegal since 1963 but is still a frequent, widespread practice—particularly for women of color. It can thrive especially in workplaces that discourage open discussion of wages and where employees fear retaliation," the report states. Even when employers are not actively discriminatory, they may rely on salary history when it comes to setting pay rates—a move that allows previous discriminatory compensation to follow women from job to job.

We certainly experienced this. Even as we moved up in the corporate ranks, the wage gap followed us.

Angelique says:

> I felt lucky for the salary I was offered, even starting in the early ranks at Pepsi, as I knew it was quite high relative to what my parents made, and therefore was just fine. My parents had always emphasized finding happiness in how you lived your life, and not in material things, and therefore I was not wired to advocate for higher compensation, but rather be grateful for the opportunities and assume that good work would lead to more opportunities, as it had for my father in his career as an engineer.
>
> However, in hindsight, I wish I had paid more attention to my compensation. It always seemed fine, I always had more than I needed for a comfortable life, and I wasn't driven by the money—I cared more about what I got to work on. But I could have also focused on the critical lessons of valuing yourself—and I find myself wanting to teach those lessons to my daughter, and also pass that guidance on to anyone I mentor or advise.

Mitzi also felt she learned this lesson over time.

I think I was a little like Angelique—pursue work that you'll enjoy and develop in first, think about the money second. Coming out of college, I thought a base salary of $2,000–$3,000 for every year of your age was good thing. Honestly, I can't remember where I got that from. I soon realized, a few years in, that that was a crazy idea and getting paid commensurate with your contribution, job description, and marketplace value was more relevant and appealing.

I've always had a passion for leading teams and businesses, so my primary career motivation has been to have a great track record of results, along with valuable skills and tools in my toolkit, so that I would have multiple career options, at any fork in the road.

Pay was important but secondary until mid-career, when all the statistics and conversations about pay inequity seemed to crescendo. For African American females, the pay gap was and still is significant. I became a lot more mindful of "being paid like Paul." I already felt like I had to work twice as hard and be twice as good, to have opportunities and experiences similar to my colleagues—getting paid 30–40 percent less seemed unfathomable. Importantly, I learned that you can do all of the research you want, but if you want to get paid like Paul, you have to start asking for what you want. I became more intentional in my discussions with my bosses about pay.

Katie talks about how she saw the wider impact of the wage gap most clearly as she moved into senior leadership roles.

> Even up to the CEO level, I was surprised to realize that it wasn't easy to ensure that all of the women on my team or in my company were being paid fairly and assessed accurately. Simply addressing inequities was difficult, as it tended to uncover repeated occurrences where a woman was judged differently than a man. There was sometimes a rational explanation for a particular point in time, but it tended to add up to a reinforcing pattern of wage gaps. There was also, at times, a real resistance to addressing it. People feared a backlash— ironically, that they would be treating the men unfairly—if they made changes.

When we reached out to the millennials and Gen Z women, they reported the same disparity—and the difficulties in fighting it. This is how one of our younger colleagues faced the issue.

> I'm guilty of it, I don't negotiate as hard for myself, I worry that it makes me look like a bitch. In fact, many people think it does. So, I actually think the advice here is really tricky. I listened to a panel where a woman entrepreneur talked about fundraising. She said: You have to recognize that the majority of entrepreneurs who've gotten VC funding are white, male, hetero, and went to an Ivy League school. That's the center of the onion. For every one of those things that you are not, that's a layer that you are away from the center. Depending how far out you are, that's the amount you should discount the advice

you are getting from the people at the center. That's where I really struggle with this issue. Because guys always tell you: you should negotiate harder! But I truly think it is received differently when you're a woman doing it. It's the worst Catch 22 because everyone's telling you to negotiate harder, and if you don't ask for it, you're not going to get it. But at the same time when you're a woman doing it, I do think men take it differently.

Meanwhile, she told us, men are having a vastly different pay negotiation experience. "We were making an offer to somebody. It was a guy. And the CEO said: Maybe we should give him more than he asked for? That would never happen with a woman. I mean, it would just never happen."

But the younger generations are pushing back.

Said one: "I am aware of the fact that women tend not to negotiate salary or approach management for promotion, or advanced pay. I've made it a point to do that. Still knowing full well, men are being paid more."

Indeed, knowledge of what everyone earns may be the key to closing the wage gap. Lily Ledbetter, a supervisor at Goodyear Tire and Rubber Co. in Gadsden, Alabama, received an anonymous note one day, revealing that she was making thousands less per year than the men in her position. That tip eventually led her to a sex discrimination case against Goodyear, her trip to the U.S. Supreme Court, and eventually, the Lily Ledbetter Fair Pay Act passed by Congress in 2009. It was a long journey through the courts and Congress. And it started with an initial act: sharing information.

Women are picking up on that act and taking it to new heights.

What the *New York Times* called the "salary whisper network" is taking hold, sharing widely the type of data that would have helped women like Lily Ledbetter negotiate for fair pay. Social media discussions like Real Media Salaries, Real Agency Salaries, and Ladies Get Paid allow women to contribute to the pay rate conversation and help each other face the pay gap hurdle with knowledge.

And knowledge is power.

If it's you . . .

Know your worth. Use the Internet and other tools to understand what others are being paid for the job you do. Does your salary measure up? If not, you've got evidence to show you're worth more. Advocate for your value. Says Angelique:

> I knew a young woman who found out that she was underpaid relative to her peers (and even versus some of the men she managed). She voiced her concern, and her manager acknowledged that they would work to close the gap. But then nothing happened. I coached her to be specific about the increase she is looking to see—and request a timeline for getting to that number. She assumed that just pointing out the issue would result in clear action, but sadly that is not often the case. It's a bit like the rule that if you need someone to call 911 in a crowd, you can't just say "someone call 911!" You have to specifically point to someone and say "you in the blue shirt, call 911" in order to make it happen.

Talk to your network. "Nurture your personal advisory board! It took me years to realize I should be asking my mentors about things like compensation," says Angelique. "When I left Pepsi to pursue other opportunities, I turned to my old friends and mentors Lori and Cie to get their advice, and it was invaluable. I should have been seeking their advice years before! I felt it was a bother, an inconvenience, but turns out, they were more than happy to help pay it forward."

Don't ding yourself in your review. We noticed as we rose into senior roles that women were much harder on themselves at review time than men. Women pointed out all their faults, all their mistakes, and created a paper trail that made it harder for them to get a raise. Meanwhile, men were more likely to record their accomplishments and sing their own praises. Dawn saw this:

> Men and women are different. I know—big insight! But when it comes to pay and perception of accomplishment and value, I do think that men have been a bit smarter than women. When CEO of Pepsi-Cola NA, I had men and women reporting to me. At review time, I noticed a difference in how the women versus the men handled their reviews. The women would come into the discussion very open to discussing what they needed to work on to get better. They knew they had accomplishments, but also areas they could strengthen.
>
> The men tended to come into the review with a point of view on what a great year they had had and when they were ready for promotion or expanded responsibilities. Opportunities for improvement were accepted. But then they wanted to talk about what next or how much of an increase they deserved.
>
> In a way, the men gave themselves the benefit of the doubt and focused on their strengths and desire to move up.

The women were more cautious and anxious to please and get better.

Neither is wrong. But since that experience I have encouraged women to enter a review able to articulate their accomplishments and view of their future capabilities. Not to dismiss opportunities to improve, embrace those. But keep the conversation focused on your career goals and strengths.

Make it easier on your manager to reward you by giving yourself a good review. Men do.

And be sure what you hear from your manager verbally matches what appears in the written review. Angelique says:

> I had an experience where my boss gave me a glowing verbal review, but when I read the language in the written evaluation, there was negative language that had never come up in the verbal review. I pressed him on it, and I was persistent until they changed the written language to match the review we discussed. I didn't know until later that others could have used that false negative review to reduce my compensation.

If you're the boss . . .

It's frustrating for women to make it into senior ranks, only to discover that even at their higher level, closing the wage gap is hard.

Says Cie:

> I found that the salary at which you bring an employee into a company will impact the rest of their tenure at the company. My experience was that annual increases usually

averaged 3 percent and promotions were often limited to 10–15 percent. So, if you hired someone on the low end of the salary range it was very difficult to get their salary up significantly. So even if someone was the most outstanding performer, it was hard to get their salary up to match a peer if that individual was brought into the company at a higher salary level. And no surprise it was usually the women who were brought in at low salary levels—often because their salary was pegged off their salary at their previous job. Once a woman starts off with a lower salary it impacts the rest of her career.

To counter the trend, we found it required an extra level of attention when it came to reviews. In Katie's experience, that's often where the justification for salaries and raises are set. Katie found watching the paperwork like a hawk was the best way to address what she was seeing as a senior leader.

> I found that I needed to pay particularly close attention to the annual review process. I would read very carefully the reviews of women when they worked for a man. There was more than one occasion when I had to point out that the actual results for a woman were being downplayed in the assessment while the opposite was happening for a man. The decades of subconscious reinforcement of gender differences were hard to overcome.

If you're the witness . . .

Allies can help close the wage gap by contributing to the conversation about salaries and adding their data to the information base. In a *Wall Street Journal* article about millennials and their comfort level discussing salaries, one white, male tech employee said he made it a point to share what he earns and also what elements of his compensation package he was able to negotiate. The way to close the gap for women and people of color is to "just be honest about what I'm making, especially as a white guy," he said.

CHAPTER 15

The Meeting Before the Meeting

What you need to know to stay in the loop

Everyone's had bad meetings, but sometimes a meeting can go particularly wrong, particularly quick. Angelique had one years ago that still spikes her blood pressure just thinking about it.

I was the new VP of Pepsi and was supposed to present my strategic plan to all the top leaders at the company, including our PepsiCo executives, our largest distributor and our head of sales. I was told that our CMO at the time had aligned the core idea of our plan with the other leaders, so the conversation would be productive.

Well, on page one, when I presented the overview of the core idea, it was clear from the faces of my audience that they were *not* on board.

I looked to the head of sales, who was supposed to be an advocate, and he said nothing. I looked to the CMO who was supposed to have laid the groundwork, and he said nothing. The meeting ground to a halt, and I felt blindsided and flustered—I thought I had done something very wrong, missed something critical to be so far off the mark.

What I learned afterwards was there were major political battles happening between these leaders, which had nothing to do with the plan I was trying to share. Shortly after that meeting, some of those leaders left the company and others were moved into new roles. There was no way I would have been able to have a successful meeting at that moment.

The dynamics of meetings are tricky. Success in a meeting involves sharp observational abilities, a keen understanding of the power relationships in the office, and no small amount of improv skills. It is a setting in which many women—even skilled, experienced women—make missteps. What should be a routine office event is often a minefield of ways a woman can stall her career.

In our collected six-corporate-sisters' experience, women are often steamrolled at meetings because they've missed a crucial step—the pre-meeting. The meetings before the meetings are the critical elements to success around the conference table. The pre-meetings have many formats. They can be casual hallway confabs. They can be private office sit-downs. They can be as simple as the five minutes of chitchat that takes place before everyone takes their seats. But these meetings-before-the-meetings are the building blocks of getting buy-in for your POV. In some cases, they are so important, the actual meeting is little more than a rubber stamp.

Mitzi, after a meeting where she felt she was blind-sided badly, had a mentor explain it to her this way: "The meeting is not just the meeting itself, it is a full trifecta: the meeting, the meeting-before-the-meeting, and oftentimes, the meeting-after-the meeting."

It is a humbling lesson many of us have learned. But the question of whether or not this is a gender issue is certainly one for discussion.

One rising leader said:

> I've definitely had the experience of being in a meeting and feeling like I've walked into the middle of a conversation that clearly started earlier and that I wasn't a part of. It makes you second guess and doubt yourself on so many levels. Why was I not included when this was discussed earlier? Was I left out on purpose or did they just forget to include me? I don't know, but it makes you doubt yourself.

124 WHAT'S UNSAID . . .

This feeling isn't exclusive to women. Certainly, if we were to poll our corporate brothers, they would be able to tell us of times they were blindsided at meetings. It happens to the best of us.

But whether or not it happens more often to women, the impact on women is outsized. While anyone can have a bad meeting, women can be more damaged by it.

Leadership consultants Jill Flynn, Kathryn Heath, and Mary Davis Holt coach women on leadership issues and they wrote the book *Break Your Own Rules* about ways women can advance in the corridors of power. Mistakes at a meeting are a primary reason women do not advance, they say. That's because meetings are the "center stage" of any company. "Meetings are the place where decisions are made and reputations are created," they wrote. Because women and people of color are scarcer in the corporate ranks, their actions in a meeting are more visible to the company at large. "Simply put, at this point in time, women have more on the line in these high-stakes interactions than their male counterparts," they wrote.

Women know this. Flynn, Heath, and Holt studied 7,000 360-degree reviews conducted on 1,100 high-ranking female executives working at the vice-president level or higher. Meetings were a clear stumbling block for women, they reported. This was true across multiple companies and industries.

We saw the same dynamic in our own work.

Says Katie:

> The idea of the meeting before the meeting is less of a gender thing specifically, but more about understanding the power dynamics in the organization. And since studies show that women aren't generally coached as much by their bosses

to learn these dynamics, not being included probably happens to more women on average. It's not a great feeling to realize that you are out of the loop and there was an entire discussion ahead of time that you weren't a part of.

What's more, it is often a no-win situation for the woman. What can you do when you realize you were out of the loop? You can shuffle quietly back to your office. That doesn't help you get your POV heard. Or you can complain, but often that doesn't go well either. Daytime TV host Kelly Ripa was blindsided when she arrived at work one day and was informed—minutes before it was publicly announced—that her co-star Michael Strahan would be leaving the show for another opportunity at the network. Shocked, Ripa took a few days off to collect her thoughts and create an action plan—behavior that drew criticism suggesting she was throwing a tantrum and behaving unprofessionally. Clearly, there was a meeting before the meeting for which Ripa did not get an invite. That fact put her at a disadvantage no matter how she reacted afterward.

How to handle the meeting before the meeting?

If it's you . . .

Perhaps the biggest step women can take towards addressing this issue is to recognize what men in the office are doing when they appear to be doing nothing—or at least nothing of value. If you've got your head down answering emails and creating PowerPoint slides, what are the men doing? Are they talking in the halls? Dropping by each other's offices? Going to lunch or for drinks after work? What seems like idle socializing may well be the meetings before the meetings you're missing. Be sure you're physically available for these conversations. Is your office door open? Are you circulating in the office having conversations? Behind a closed door or with your earphones in, you may be walling yourself off from the critical pre-meeting interactions.

While pre-meetings can take place weeks, days, and hours before the official meeting, connecting even a few minutes beforehand can pay off. Something as innocuous as five minutes of pre-meeting small talk can have an impact. This is especially true for individuals who may have trouble getting a word in during the meeting. A study published in the *Journal of Managerial Psychology* found a strong link between pre-meeting communication and the meeting's effectiveness. The positive impact is strongest for those who score low in extraversion, the study said.

The trick, says Katie, is to learn the particular dynamics of your company. "Try and build trusted relationships across departments and up and down levels to give you a better sense of how things operate. Understanding the power dynamics and decision-making dynamics is critical in most organizations and it's rarely presented to you in a PowerPoint," she says.

One of our Gen Z colleagues also offered this tip, courtesy of new technology in the workplace. She routinely scans the public virtual calendars of her colleagues and managers, to see who is meeting with whom and on what topic. Most calendars default to public mode, she said. It's a good way to see if there's a meeting going on that you ought to be in.

There are also steps you can take if you're in the meeting and you become aware that there was a pre-meeting to which you were not privy.

Dawn says:

Have you ever been in a meeting where the discussion goes quickly and a potentially hot subject seems to get resolved without a lot of discussion? This is likely the result of the "meeting before the meeting" designed to control the decision and align a key group ahead of time. Frankly, this happened frequently at the NFL. Senior leadership would often not get a chance to weigh in on a tough topic for fear that discussion of it would leak to the press. Well, first of all: change the team if you cannot trust them. Secondly, if you are in the room do not let it proceed as a "rubber stamp" meeting. Ask a question requiring someone to explain their POV. You will likely be joined by someone else in the room who did not feel up to speed and hopefully more discussion will ensue. You are not being disruptive, rather making sure all sides have been evaluated and perhaps a new, better solution is offered.

Keep this tactic for use on important, rather than routine issues, Dawn says. When it's a routine matter, the pre-meeting/rubber stamp process may be fine, even more efficient. "But if it is about a major move, a major reputational question, you are paid to participate. Just do it in a questioning innocent way, not with any angry tone."

Cie has an internal checklist for ensuring she's "pre-wired" for meetings: "The more important the meeting, the more pre-wiring needed; the more senior people involved the more pre-wiring needed: the more cross-functional teams involved the more pre-wiring needed; the bigger budget consideration the more pre-wiring needed."

It all falls under the heading *"Be prepared,"* says Mitzi.

Flynn, Holt, and Heath talk about the challenges women face. I think that's magnified even more for women of color. Throughout my career, as the only one or one of a handful of women of color in the room or on a team, I've felt like I've been on the center stage with all the spotlights and microphones on me, with every move noticed. Learning how things work and who works them has been paramount for me. My advice: be proactive. I've found that the best defense against being left out of meetings before meetings is a good offense. I started seeking out and initiating pre-meetings so I wouldn't be blindsided and because I found it to be a very effective way to understand the multiple POVs and objections ahead of time, when I could do something about them.

One more tip: Don't forget the post-meeting. Some companies have formal processes around meeting notes with very specific to-dos identified so everyone knows what to do next. Others schedule postmortems after big meetings and yet others favor more of a "curbside debrief" to take place in the halls. Ask the questions ahead of time to learn how your company works and how to maximize your effectiveness within the company culture. Says Mitzi: "While not talked about as much, I think the meeting after the meeting is important also. It's usually where you get the postmortem on key next steps, who landed their points, what worked, what didn't. It is the time when people get to clarify and/or amplify their point with the senior leader or the meeting owner. This meeting often takes place during the walk from the conference room back to the office or to the next meeting. Women really lose when this last conversation ends in the men's restroom. Are you the first to leave the meeting or the Zoom room? Beware!

If you're the boss . . .

Mentor and train for meeting-before-the-meeting skills. Don't assume everyone already knows how to do it.

Says Angelique:

> I recall observing a really successful male executive at Pepsi who used to have a great track record at large, difficult meetings getting his ideas accepted. When I worked for him and it was our project that needed to land, I remember him introducing me to the term "pre-wiring." He literally made the rounds to each stakeholder prior to the meeting and presented his case and was able to hear and address any concerns. By the time we got to the large session, everyone was "pre-wired" to understand the idea and realize all their concerns were addressed.

You can also consider formalizing the meeting-before-the-meeting process in your company or team. Lori experienced this in one of her post-Pepsi jobs.

"There was literally a parallel track for every key meeting," says Lori.

> When we had key meetings upcoming with the CEO, we had to organize a full set of formal pre-meetings to align the key stakeholders and get their sworn oath that they would

be supportive in the meeting with the CEO, even if things got heated. You have to make sure to specifically ask people if they were going to support you when things got ugly in the room (as they often did). Once, we had a very big, cross-functional, very controversial project we were taking to the CEO for approval. We knew it would be a tense and difficult meeting, and we would have some naysayers in the room. We were pre-aligning with the head of our business unit, and at the end of the meeting, he said, "Okay, I'm with you '*win or tie*.'" While I *think* he was just joking, it taught me a valuable lesson about how hard it really is to get someone who is truly on your side, versus being on your side only if it's easy.

One way to take pre-meetings out of the shadows and into public view is to give the process a name, says Lori. Maybe something cute, like the Pre-Game. But a phrase that you can use as a leader that names and discusses the meetings that take place before The Meeting. In that way, newcomers will be able to see the process more clearly.

Dawn also sees codifying the pre-meeting as part of a leader's job.

I think that pre-meetings naturally occur when a topic is important and people talk ahead of a meeting. As the boss, if you know a pre-meeting has occurred and not everyone in the meeting was at the pre-discussion, start the meeting by getting people up to speed. Acknowledge a key issue that people casually discussed ahead of time. Share that discussion and ask if there are any additional thoughts or perspectives. Call on people not in the pre-meeting to encourage their contributions.

If you're the witness . . .

If there's a meeting-before-the-meeting subculture at your office, speak its name. Too often women miss the signals and there is little open discussion of the power dynamics that lead up to meeting success. If you're the witness, you have the opportunity to take this process out of the shadows. Tell a newcomer how it's done. Alert a colleague as to who might be important pre-meeting targets for conversation. This is what happened to Angelique after her meeting from hell. "The incoming CMO did this for me. He found me immediately after that awful meeting and explained what was happening so I could see that I hadn't screwed up—there were politics at work. While it didn't save me in the moment with that very career-making-or-breaking audience, it did keep me from quitting, and I learned my first of many hard lessons about executive politics."

CHAPTER 16

Bad Assumptions

The wrong ideas that hold women back

I f you rise into the ranks of senior management at a mid-size or large company, you may be asked to participate in a routine ritual known as the talent meeting. That's a benign-sounding title for a gathering of epic consequences. Talent meetings are where fates are decided.

In any given talent meeting, the powerful will determine who will move up in the ranks of the company. Promotions will be discussed. New assignments will be debated. Individuals will be matched—or not—with their new roads forward. And all around the table, the talk will focus on the very human details of those not present: Who is ready to move up? Who needs more time in their current job? Who will best fit a plum new assignment? Talent meetings are portals to the next level.

And if that's not consequential enough, these gatherings are also often quicksand for women. That's because talent meetings are often infected with a practice that stops women's advancement: Bad Assumptions.

Bad assumptions are a mindset. They are a set of beliefs that infiltrate the workplace and play in the background when decisions like who should get the London assignment are discussed. They can crop up anywhere in a company—from talent meetings to board rooms to office chats. Bad assumptions are ordinary information about an individual that becomes unconsciously weaponized—often before the impacted person has any idea.

Bad assumptions don't sound all that bad when you hear them.

"She has two small kids."

"Her husband just made partner."

"She just got engaged."

But when they come up in places like a talent meeting, they become bricks in the wall.

"She can't handle a promotion. She has two small kids."

"She won't move to London. Her husband just made partner at his job."

"She's not a good pick to handle the new account. She just got engaged. She'll be distracted this year."

Keep in mind that none of those things—small children, a successful spouse, an upcoming wedding—would be used to hinder a man's advancement.

Bad assumptions are where gender bias meets the talent plan. Even when the woman brings all the right skills to the job, the bad assumptions can stop her. And she may not even know it happened.

In some ways, bad assumptions are more damaging than actual bad actors. You may battle against a single bad boss or even a team that can't seem to accept gender equality. But how do you deal with assumptions that waft into the workplace undetected and linger in the back of the minds of decision makers, popping out in places where you don't see or hear them, having their negative impact in ways you may never understand? Bad assumptions strike quietly, even silently, and that makes them doubly difficult to defeat.

Bad assumptions are not just something men wander into. Women traffic in bad assumptions, too. All the time.

Worse, bad assumptions are not the exception. They are the rule.

We saw it play out routinely as we moved in our own corporate lanes.

Cie's view:

> I used to participate in annual "people planning" meetings where the senior team would review the entire marketing department for promotions and assignment rotations. For each individual, we reviewed their accomplishments,

strengths, weaknesses, tenure in current role, and critical experiences and balanced all of these against the needs of the business. Out of our process we would come up with a short list for each position. It was common for the senior team (both men and women) not to put women with young children on the short list for positions requiring heavy travel or relocation.

We would make assumptions about the women such as:

"Jane has two kids in middle school. There is no way she can fly to the Texas every week"

"Jane's husband is a successful attorney tied to the New York office she can't move to Florida"

How did we know what was happening in Jane's personal life?

Maybe Jane was the primary breadwinner and her husband took the lead with the kids. Maybe Jane and her husband think New York is too expensive and would love to move. Maybe Jane's husband wants to retire. Maybe Jane has elderly parents in Florida and moving there would be ideal. Maybe Jane and her husband are separated and the kids live with her husband during the week. Maybe they are about to get a divorce. Who knows??

Only Jane.

But Jane was not in the meeting. It was just the people-planning team—and their assumptions.

Research suggests that these specific assumptions around women in the workforce often stem from more broadly held stereotypes of women in general. *Harvard Business Review* took a look at this phenomenon and how it plays out in the workplace. The problem, wrote authors Catherine H. Tinsley and Robin J. Ely, is that on a societal level, we assume biological differences that don't exist. That leads to assumptions such as women lack the desire to negotiate or women lack confidence. These are all untrue, the authors say, yet they linger in the workplace as stereotypes that are embraced and leveraged by men and women alike.

Assumptions have real impact in the workplace. A study by Boston Consulting Group found that women start their careers with as much ambition as men when it comes to the desire to hold leadership positions or be promoted. But ambition is influenced by company culture and the assumptions that weave through it. BCG measured the percentage of people aged 30–40 who desired a promotion or leadership role. In companies that make gender diversity a priority, 85 percent of women desired a promotion (compared with 87 percent of men). In companies that failed to embrace gender diversity as a corporate value, just 66 percent of women said they wanted a promotion, compared with 83 percent of the men. Critics may use the data of the second company to promote the concept that women are less ambitious than men and simply don't want promotions. But we argue that's an assumption—and one that creates an air of discouragement around advancement that is difficult to battle.

Bad assumptions aren't just leveled at married women or mothers. "One bad assumption I'd like to call out is assuming that single women do not have personal lives to manage just like married women or parents," says Angelique.

> I was helping a young, high potential female leader negotiate a relocation to a new office. The HR lead suggested that she needed to have a "good reason" such as her spouse being

relocated. I pushed back: why the double standard, to assume that single people don't need to manage their personal lives? Doesn't their personal network have just as much impact as someone who is married? And the HR lead immediately related. She recalled that when she was single, she was given weekend work "because she didn't have a family" and she resented it. Here was her chance to set the right standard, and she did. They approved the young woman's relocation.

The impact of bad assumptions is one that permeates the lives of the next generation of leaders. Our millennial and Gen Z colleagues see the practice in their everyday work lives.

> I saw it happen to my boss. She's a mom of three kids. When the company was expanding, there was an account that would have required more long-distance travel. She was a good fit for the account but she didn't get it—she got another one that, frankly, didn't make as much sense for her portfolio. You have to wonder if they would have given her husband that account? Obviously, he has three kids, too. But would they have thought about it that way?

One of our interviewees wondered if she'd even been bogged down in bad assumptions herself. When hiring at the junior level, she wondered, was she influenced by the candidate with the flashy engagement ring and the talk of plans for a big wedding? "Was I thinking that she's not a good hire because she's going through a big wedding and I need the team to be focused?"

We've had those moments ourselves.

Katie says:

> I have had to catch myself at times during possible lay-
> off conversations to not factor in the "but he's providing for
> a family" reason to keep some guy off the list. Unconscious
> (or semi-conscious) bias is deep rooted and I certainly
> know I've been guilty of it. This is why having real diversity
> in decision-making situations is important—we need to chal-
> lenge each other and make sure our own unconscious biases
> are being called out and addressed.

Assumptions are sneaky little buggers. They drift into our thinking
when we least expect it.

How do you battle a threat that is so hard to pin down?

If it's you . . .

Be open about what you want—and what you don't want. Don't
assume anyone knows you want the hot new account with a ton of
travel or the challenging assignment that will demand long hours or
the management position that will take you out of your comfort zone.
If you want these things, articulate them. The assumptions in the talent meeting may not be in your favor. Ensure there is another story—
the story you want to tell—running the background of the decision-
makers' minds.

Too often, women make their own bad assumption—that if they
put their heads down and work furiously, they will eventually be
noticed for their efforts and promoted. If that's not happening for you,
consider your assumptions—and the ones your manager holds. If you

have not made it clear to others what you want, don't assume they'll be able to figure it out.

If you're the boss . . .

Be aware of the assumptions and challenge them.

Dawn says:

> We need to ask men and women what they are willing to consider and not make assumptions. And these questions need to be specific. Not: Would you be willing to move to the West Coast? Instead: I have an opportunity for you to run a sizable business. But it would require moving to the West Coast. Now that will get someone to think hard. Not the casual question. And we should not have unconscious bias the other way and assume the man will move. He may have extended family responsibilities on the East Coast and not be as mobile as another woman. Each case and each person is different. And timing matters. So just ask and do not assume.

What's more, be ready to challenge the assumptions when you hear them. Says Katie:

> In one people-planning session there was a talented young woman who was a new mother and we were discussing her best next role. I was running the cola brands at the time and it was an intense group with a lot of long hours. When it was suggested that she would not be a good fit there given her family responsibilities, I pushed back and said that I did not want

our top talent to miss out on a good role because we couldn't accommodate a working mother. She joined the team and was a great contributor.

Project the belief that your employee will succeed, says Angelique.

Think of it as a parallel to the self-perception theory. Just think about how confident you would be if your boss gave you the benefit of the doubt and pro-actively treated you like a superstar! I'm reminded of the "claquers" of eighteenth-century France who were hired to lead vigorous applause at theaters to make everyone else more enthusiastic about what they were seeing—and it worked!

If you're the witness . . .

Question the narrative. Do you hear people say that women lack ambition? Or that they avoid conflict? Or that they lose their desire for promotions and challenges when they become mothers? As a witness, you're in a position to challenge those assumptions. Try: What makes you say that? Or: Did you hear that from the woman herself or are you just assuming? Casual interactions between colleagues can have an impact on the bad assumption landscape.

Another option: generate a plausible alternative. If you're the witness to the conversation that goes:

"Jane didn't say a word in today's meeting. She lacks the fire for promotion."

You have the opportunity to offer a counter assumption. Try: "Maybe. Or maybe she's tired of speaking up only to have Greg say the same thing five minutes later and get the credit."

And then go ask Jane about the meeting. Ask her about her lack of participation. She may have information that will add to the understanding of what happened.

Fill the gap between fact and assumption. It's wider than we think.

CHAPTER 17

Counting the Room

How it feels to be the only

When you look around your workplace, how many people do you see who look like you?

If you're a white man, perhaps this counting process never even occurred to you.

But if you're not, it's probably a reality that you ponder regularly.

This is the process that is known colloquially as "counting the room." One faction in the office does this all the time, at the morning meeting or the team lunch or the industry trade show. The other never does this. Counting the room is an alien concept. What's the point of the exercise?

When you have this much disparity—every day versus never—the disparity breeds an enormous understanding gap. Neither side can relate to the other on this topic.

When it comes to discussing diversity, equity, and inclusion issues, one of the most difficult concepts to convey to a majority is how it feels to be under-represented—to be the only person who looks like you in the office, at the conference table, in the C-suite. When you are in the majority, you may hardly notice the number of women and/or people of color around you. But if you are in the minority—or alone—you notice it all the time, as a matter of course.

This is true whether you're at your entry-level job or running the show.

Angelique has been a CMO, led global brands, and advised several start-ups. Ask her about counting the room.

She says:

> OMG, I count the room *all the time*. Like a tic, I just can't help it. Calculate the percentage—and it is rarely above 30 percent. And then try for women of color, and the math is too easy because the numerator is always so small. It's like I'm calculating my odds of success.
>
> So why are all these talented, successful women feeling the need to count the room? And probably more importantly,

why aren't the men counting the room and seeing something is wrong? I'm guessing because they don't know what being outnumbered feels like. What decisions are altered because of those numbers? What ideas are not offered because the person doesn't feel they will be understood?

When you count the room, it gives a data point to the feeling you carry about being on the outside, looking in. The visual is a reminder that you are not among your kind. It is a constant calculation you run, like checking the temperature outside to see what the weather will be like any given day. When you count the room, you check its temperature. How warm will it be in here? How chilly? The numbers will give you a preview of the climate you'll experience in that moment.

That we found ourselves counting the room in our younger days was not surprising. The fact that we still do it—now when nearly half the workforce is female—is a testament to just how slowly change emerges. We are half the workforce, yet we are outnumbered in offices and leadership roles and boardrooms. For women seeking to move up into power positions, it's still far too easy to count the room and see that math adds up to another barrier to advancement.

Research shows us that when you're out-numbered, that impacts your ability to succeed. *Frontiers in Psychology* published a study conducted by researchers in The Netherlands, focusing on the experience of women in STEM careers. They found that women in the male-dominated work environments experienced a high level of gender identity threat—the feeling of being devalued or stigmatized at work on the basis of gender. This resulted in lower confidence and weaker work engagement compared with their male peers. Even more concerning, the study revealed that women in these highly male environments often seek to self-protect by downplaying the role of gender altogether. They seek to assimilate into the masculine culture. They don't support (and even sometimes oppose) collective attempts to bolster the status of women in their workplace. They don't step up to serve as role models or mentors for female STEM students. And when interviewed about their accomplishments, they tend to downplay or ignore the significance of gender in their career trajectory.

Indeed, already outnumbered in the room, these women sought to shrink their female presence even further as a defensive strategy.

TrustRadius, a technology review site based in Austin, Texas, conducts an annual survey on the experience of women in the technology sector. Their 2021 findings: the majority of women working in the technology sector (72 percent) say they are regularly outnumbered by men in business meetings by at least a 2:1 ratio. Just over one-quarter of the women say that ratio is 5:1. Their thin ranks create hurdles. They are four times more likely than men to see gender bias as an obstacle to promotion. The vast majority believe they have to work harder than their male co-workers to "prove their worth." And their ability to impact their corporate environment is stymied—72 percent say they work in an office in which "bro culture" is pervasive. That can mean everything from an uncomfortable work environment to sexual harassment and assault.

Having few women in the room has an impact, not just on the current female workforce, but the future prospects for better diversity and inclusion. When women in tech consider their professional futures, the TrustRadius survey noted, they scan the office and see few role models for moving up. The study captured this concern when it asked women to envision their futures with the organization: two-thirds felt there was no clear path forward for them. At least, not one they could envision when they looked around the office.

Lest you brush this off as a STEM issue, the annual McKinsey Women in the Workplace survey shows the breadth of the problem. The "Women in the Workplace" report analyzed HR data from 279 companies. It also harvested survey responses from sixty-four thousand full-time employees from eighty-one companies. Across industries, women are counting the room. About one-fifth of women in the McKinsey survey say they're frequently the only woman in the room. Women who are "onlys" in their work environments are more likely to report microaggressions. And they feel the pressure of their small numbers. "With everyone's eyes on them, women Onlys can be heavily scrutinized and held to higher standards," the report found.

We certainly observed that.

Says Cie:

> One of the games I have played with myself over the years is to calculate the percentage of women in meetings at work. Sometimes the math was not too challenging, as many times it was only me. The math got slightly trickier when there were three women in a room with forty-one people. Regardless, the prevailing answer was usually less than 30 percent and when I factored out administrative staff, the number was generally below 20 percent.
>
> I thought gender calculation was unique to me, but I came to learn that female representation in 1) meetings, 2) task forces, 3) senior positions, 4) etc., is something that *many, many* women pay very close attention to.

Says Mitzi:

Cie mentions the counting games she was able to play relative to women attending meetings, being on task forces, and occupying leadership roles. For a long time, I could only wish that the African American female representation in a room was ripe for counting and percentage calculating. I can think of numerous times when I was simply happy to see another African American female in the same meeting room. Early in my corporate tenure, there were only a few VPs in sales and marketing who were women of color. Unfortunately, the picture wasn't any better on the customer side either. As dire and difficult as it seemed, I stayed focused on contributing and having impact at the most senior level possible so that other WOC would have more opportunity to do the same.

Our younger counterparts tell the same story.

Said one: "How often do I count the room? Every single time because, in my work situation, I'm usually the only woman and the only woman of color. Or if I'm in a room full of women, I'm the only woman of color. Once I was at a conference and I was the only woman of color at the whole conference. And I was the one presenting."

Said another: "I am often the only woman. I always make a mental note."

Zoom use during the COVID pandemic only seemed to heighten the realization that as women, they were outnumbered. "You looked at the squares of people on your screen and realized how few of them were women," said one of our millennial colleagues. "It was staring us right in the face."

How can we counter the counting?

If it's you . . .

Understand and label the process as part of your tactical effort, says Angelique. "I realize I may be doing it because I am calculating what tactics I have to employ in order to be heard. When the room is even, I am able to relax and be myself. When I'm the only woman, I am on guard for behaviors I've seen way too many times."

But fight the impulse to let the numbers back you off. Says Katie:

> I'm definitely more self-conscious in a situation when I'm vastly outnumbered and I feel pressure to contribute and be viewed as a valuable addition. Depending on my comfort level with the meeting topic or the attendees, it probably makes me more cautious and reserved than I realize, which then might reinforce any existing biases against women and their value at the table.

If you're the boss . . .

Make counting the room a business metric. Says Katie: "Count the room yourself! Know that every woman and person of color in the room is doing the same thing. Spend a month writing it down for every meeting or conversation and see what it looks like at the end. Then make changes if you don't like what you see."

Take seriously the impact of hiring and mentoring. Ensure that the women in your ranks see "a path forward" when they count the room—that is, people who look like them in senior jobs.

Says Cie:

> We need women in the workplace to be mentored to ensure they are promoted at the same pace as the young men (especially their first promotion).
>
> We need women to be able to look up in their organization and see female role models in key leadership positions.
>
> We need the business world to ensure women, even if less well known, are given equal opportunities.
>
> We need women to look out for each other and champion each other.
>
> We need women to be proactive and advocate for themselves in salary and promotion discussions.
>
> We need women to take risks on other women.
>
> We need women to take more risks on themselves—apply for jobs even if you do not fulfill 100 percent of job specifications.

Look for ways to highlight the issue to others, recommends Lori. "When someone says that Sally didn't add a lot to the conversation at the last staff meeting, say, 'I'm sure it's intimidating being one of only two women on a 12-person leadership team. What could *we* do to make her feel comfortable and make sure we hear her voice? We hired her for her great skill and talent; let's put some of the burden on *us* to make sure she can thrive.'"

Remember, too, that counting doesn't only happen in a conference room or office. Think of other places a woman or person of color might note representation, says Angelique. "As someone who has organized many thought leadership events, I always insist that the speaker lineup be diverse. And it's not good enough for the women to be in the role of moderator. I want the audience to look across the speaker slate and not see a sea of white men."

If you're the witness . . .

Count the room yourself! If you're in the majority and you've never felt the need to calculate the percentage of space your gender or race occupy around any given conference table, start now. Count the women. Count the people of color. Do the math. How outnumbered are those individuals? What are you doing to ensure their voices are not drowned out by the majority? What steps are you taking to include those individuals in the conversation, in the decision making, in the power structure?

Consider putting yourself in a situation in which you are outnumbered to see how it feels. Get a manicure. Take a yoga class. When you notice you are the only one of *you* in the space, how does that affect you?

Counting the room does not need to remain limited to those in the minority. If everyone did it, we might make a lot more progress.

CHAPTER 18

Man-Centives

From polo shirts to cigars, how incentives tend to incentivize men

Thank you!

How do you prefer to hear that sentiment in your workplace?

The practice of rewards and incentives is a complex business. Managers realize that expressing thanks for a job well done is critical to morale. But how those thanks are expressed can be a minefield. What is a desirable prize to one may be a dud—or even an insult—to another.

When the issue of gender comes into play, the process becomes even more fraught. Research suggests men and women have very different ideas of what constitutes an appropriate workplace thank-you. And despite that, so many traditional incentives are designed with men in mind. They can range from plaques to trips to cigars.

Few workplace rewards programs are designed for the employee who is racing the clock to get to daycare pickup, planning an evening of homework supervision, and wondering if anyone at the company notices her input. Even with women at 50 percent of the workforce, incentives often fail to reflect that audience.

For Cie, it was the parade of golf shirts that got to her.

I must have received over forty men's golf shirts from my corporate days. I always thought it was such a letdown to get a gift and realize it was a shirt designed for a man, sized for a man, and intended for a man. I noticed the other women were so used to it they would reply "my husband will love this."No company would ever consider giving a man a woman's shirt in a size small, but the reverse happened year in and year out during my career. How hard would it be to get both a man's and a woman's version of a shirt?

Angelique recalls being allowed to choose her reward was not always easier. "For my five-year anniversary at PepsiCo, I got to select a reward from a catalog—and I selected a power drill. I don't think I ever used that power drill, but from all the options, that seemed to have the best possibility of use. It surely reminded me that the catalog was not designed with me in mind."

Research suggests men and women see workplace rewards differently. A study by the American Psychological Association found both men and women valued recognition on the job, but while 54 percent of men said they were satisfied with their employer's recognition practices, only 46 percent of women agreed. About 52 percent of men said the recognition system was fair, versus 42 percent of women. About 56 percent of men said their supervisor doled out recognition effectively, versus 47 percent of women.

Perhaps the most complicated thank-you is cold, hard cash. Researchers Hanna M. Sittenthaler and Alwine Mohnene looked into the ways incentives landed for men and women. Their findings, published in the *Journal of Business Economics* presented a surprising picture. When asked, both men and women said they'd prefer a cash incentive. But in practice, when men and women were placed into groups for the tournament-style academic experiment, men were clearly motivated best by cash, whereas women performed better when the prize was non-monetary—such as, in this study, a box of specialty chocolates.

"The gender differences in the effectiveness of monetary and non-monetary incentives do not seem to be triggered by the perceived attractiveness of the non-monetary incentives but rather by the differences between men and women in feelings of appreciation and perceived performance pressure in a tournament setting," they wrote. "Therefore, our results indicate that gender differences must be considered when implementing incentives."

A poorly chosen gift can be a true let down. One of our millennial colleagues had this experience during the pandemic: much of her team had been furloughed. The company kept only the top performers on her team—all women. Management sent all of them a care package. "Which was so nice of them! But when I got it, everything was just so masculine. Golf polos, this really masculine backpack, everything. I thought: well, this goes in my Goodwill pile." It was particularly troubling she said, since it was well-known that hers was an all-female team.

What you can do?

If it's you . . .

If the incentive you've received is less than incentivizing, speak up. It may be that no one's ever mentioned it before. If the prize for the top performer of the quarter is a trip that you couldn't take or an activity you'd never consider fun, suggest other options that might be more inclusive. If it's a plaque or cash, accept graciously and put in your suggestions for future rewards. Incentives can often arise out of corporate traditions—traditions that extend back before a time when the workforce had women in sufficient numbers. If you're in a position to be rewarded for top performance, you're in a positive light at that moment in time. Take the opportunity to express how the incentive program can be updated to meet the changing workforce.

If you're the boss . . .

Some of the ways to make rewards more inclusive are easy—make sure the team t-shirts come in men's and women's styles, edit competitions so that they use inclusive language (avoid "Salesman of the Year," "Superman," etc.). Time celebrations so that working parents can participate.

Some take more time. Consider a redesign of your rewards program and include women in the redesign team. Open a discussion. Ask your team what sorts of incentives would be most welcome? Which ones end up in the Goodwill pile?

But don't give up on the old rewards entirely. Encourage women to recognize their own contributions. Men do. Push female employees to post more of their work and accomplishments on office community platforms like Slack and WhatsApp groups. When they do so, endorse and amplify their contributions.

And don't let any object stand in for actually expressing your thanks. Katie says:

> Don't forget the power of a simple personalized note (preferably handwritten). I kept a file of personal notes I've received. It was something that was a morale booster when I needed it. My boss at ESPN was a master of the handwritten note. He was so good at it and always had a stack of personalized note cards ready to go. You sometimes forget when you

get to be the boss how meaningful a note that just says "great job on XYZ project" means to people. And how quick and easy it is to do.

Dawn also advises a strategy that isn't just focused on physical gifts, but mixed with positive comments and notes. Often, she says, those are the thank-yous that are truly incentivizing.

If you're the witness . . .

Look around at the winners in the office—the ones who get the most recognition and applause. Is that a diverse group? Does it reflect the overall workforce? If not, you're in a position to start the conversation about why that is the case. Why is the top sales performer always a man? Why are there never any women's names on the recognition plaques?

And speak up about golf shirts, says Cie. "Old habits die hard. If you hear of someone planning an incentives program, proactively suggest non-gendered awards or male and female options with appropriate sizing."

Section Four

Fun and Games, Workplace Style

Not every workplace interaction happens in the workplace. Plenty happens in after-work social-izing or on organized work outings and retreats. These are interactions that used to be all male and now are co-ed. These extra-office encounters are the genesis of some of our funniest stories—and most infuriating interactions. They make great war stories, and we share them to shed light on this important and often under-discussed factor in career success.

CHAPTER 19

Saddle Up!

Surviving male-oriented company outings

Standing on a boat dock at 4:30 a.m., Katie pondered her situation—and her choices.

It was the morning of a company fishing outing. Katie knew well that this particular senior executive loved to deep sea fish and that he often invited others in the company to go with him. "When I got the call that he wanted to take me and my team out one summer day, I took a deep breath and said 'sure!,'" she recalls. "I would absolutely not, in a hundred years, ever choose to do this on my own time. But I knew it was the right thing to do and I hoped that once I had enough coffee it might even be fun."

The word "fun" does not appear in Katie's description of the rest of the day. Indeed, the phrases "brutally long" and "wasn't so bad" stand out as her emotional takeaways. But from a business perspective, Katie was clear. "It created both a bonding opportunity and a lifetime memory of being way out by the gulf stream and actually catching a fish. It did feel a little like I passed a test. I was happy we did it."

Outings are tricky territory for women. They're supposed to be fun—certainly the men who designed them and have been enjoying them for years think so. The outings, which can be one-day events like Katie's fishing trip or multi-day retreats—often involve activities that traditionally appeal to men such as fishing, hunting, sports (as a spectator or participant), even alcohol and cigars. Not to say women can't like these things. Plenty of women do. But taking the broad perspective, it's not uncommon for outings to feature activities that, to paraphrase Katie, many women wouldn't choose in a hundred years. That makes the corporate outing less of a fun time away from the office and more like a rite of passage. They are tests that demand a passing grade.

There's not a lot of academic studies on the subject of male-centric business outings. The topic of outings overall gets plenty of attention. Spending time away from the office with colleagues offers a chance to get to know people on a more personal level. Connections and friendships are made when the time spent talking is longer than the five minutes between meetings. Outings are also often important milestones in a corporate year. They are events that take place regularly and new employees are assimilated into the culture by participating and sharing in the corporate traditions. For existing male leadership, welcoming women into the activities of the annual retreat are a positive step—a way to promote inclusivity. While researchers can agree that these events are opportunities to bond and advance one's corporate career, they are silent on the problem presented by male-preferred activities.

But while science may not have tackled this topic yet, others are certainly filling the void. The popular blog "Ask A Manager" fields this issue frequently. In the Q and A format, a former office chief-of-staff Alison Green has advised many workers who faced unexpected gender bias in the company outing. There was the manager whose company had long organized an annual golf outing—but none of the female managers played golf. Should the event be canceled? There was the IT professional—the lone woman on her team—who didn't know how to respond when the team holiday luncheon was booked at Hooters.

And another who planned to abstain from the outing planned at a gun range—until her boss asked her directly if she'd be going. Is declining a career-killer?

Outings, like casual sexist language, are not "nothing." They are infrequent and may seem optional. But many companies take their annual traditions and outings seriously. And many men take their efforts to include women in their outings as a positive move on their part. Saying no may not be an option.

When we received invitations to the outings, we went, no matter what they were doing.

Like the time Mitzi made her first attempt at riding a snowmobile.

> I wanted to be a team player, so I participated—though I was apprehensive. As a first timer, I feared getting left behind in the middle of nowhere and/or getting stuck. My bad for putting those thoughts out there—I ended up flipping over and had to get help to get turned right side up. I was so embarrassed! Fortunately, no one mentioned it. I guess I got credit for trying on that one.

She also continued her process of participating, even if she'd never done the activity before. Her bid to join the hunting outing went better.

> I had heard several stories from colleagues about the joys of hunting with Pepsi distributors. All the stories made it sound like an awesome bonding and "rites of passage" experience. So, when my team and I went on a market tour with one of the Pepsi distributors known also for their hunting, I asked them when there might be an opportunity for us to hunt. To which

they replied, "How about this afternoon?" So, we spent the afternoon hunting. Starting out, I had no idea what I was doing and felt slightly uncomfortable holding a loaded gun. Afterward, though not a marksman by any stretch of the imagination, I knew how to hold a gun and shoot. A good relationship got even better—as I was vulnerable and willing to learn and explore. They were willing to share and teach. We both had a wonderful experience and more stories for future conversations.

Mitzi had a little more enthusiasm for her rite of passage than Cie, who really just wanted to get through it without hurting herself or another living creature. This took place on the "fun" day of the week-long work retreat:

The group activity day was one of the longest days in my life. It is hard to find a sport I do not like—but I am terrified of riding horses because I had a bad fall when I was a kid. And I think fishing is cruel. Unfortunately, our bonding day activity consisted of three hours on horseback to get to a river to fly fish and then three hours horseback riding to return. I did not want to seem like a buzzkill so I opted not to mention my fear of horses or my disgust of fishing. My horse immediately figured out that I was scared and proceeded to spend the entire day grazing for food. One of the guides quickly saw my fear and hung back with me. So, I made it—but those six hours of horseback riding felt like twelve hours. We were taught to cast fly fish lines and then we all spread out along the river. I found a sequestered place and never even tried to cast my line—I was the only person who did not catch a fish. I don't think this issue is unique to women. I have heard stories from men on this topic as well. There are guys who feel pressure to "man up" and hunt. Being more sensitive about this dynamic will benefit everyone.

Dawn can top that story. She attended a similar retreat—seven months pregnant. Dawn waded into the water with everyone else during the fishing part of the expedition—the size of her belly did not go unnoticed.

But that was just the daytime activity. At night, there was organized group drinking. "Sambuca Patrol was mandatory," Dawn said. "No one ever said this out loud, but you just knew. Folklore from the company's colorful past would be passed down and it was a rite of passage. And [the CEO] noted who was there." Dawn found the stories were a lot less funny when you weren't drinking. And staying up that late was not easy. "I think I made it to 3 a.m. But I would not have missed it to understand what others frequently talked about. My advice: when company folklore and tradition are involved, even if not 'up to the times,' try to find a way to participate to keep yourself on the inside. You would be respected for sure if you choose not to go, but you would also be making yourself inadvertently on the outside of the circle."

On a separate trip, Dawn made sure she was in the circle, even when it meant going pheasant hunting with a bad case of strep throat (she bagged a bird before retreating to the bus) and sitting in on an after-dinner cigar session when pregnant. "At least they were trying to include me. I sure wished there had been the after-dinner chocolate-making class instead."

Our millennial and Gen Z sisters told us this continues to be a challenge. And it can get dicey:

What I find the hardest is that these dinners and happy hours for men in my business are something that are easy and normal. For me, they are a real challenge that I have to mentally and physically deal with while keeping cool and collected with all of the flowing alcohol. As a small person and a woman, I cannot drink as much as my colleagues, so at a dinner where we have four courses, I can't drink four glasses of wine or I will be on the floor and then will also lose credibility with my clients/suppliers. As a woman, if I were to get even slightly tipsy, I would be labeled as sloppy and unprofessional while men can get super drunk and it's completely acceptable. In addition to this, dinners and outings are also something that could potentially become an uncomfortable situation for me. As people begin to drink, their inhibitions are lifted and I have been petted, pulled onto a man's lap, invited to bedrooms, and by people that I thought I trusted. I have had to find a way to navigate uncomfortable and potentially dangerous situations by cutting out dinners and happy hours. I leave early or do not do them. This then limits my opportunity to network and reinforce relationships, but I feel safe that way and I will not put myself into those uncomfortable settings. So, I just have to deal with that handicap.

Mitzi developed a system to address this particular challenge.

In the industries that I've worked in, a lot of networking and relationship building happened at happy hours and dinners. If there was a happy hour before dinner, I would often arrive at the happy hour midway through and transition to dinner. If there was just a reception or an after-dinner cocktail hour, I would order a club soda with a twist of lime and network with intention. I would employ my three Ws: walk in, walk around to talk and engage with all key stakeholders, and walk out. It was important to show up and connect.

How can you handle the outings that seem to be organized with guys in mind?

If it's you . . .

Give the activity your best effort—and then volunteer to be on the planning committee for future events. There's no reason activities can't be planned that appeal broadly to men and women. It may well be that no one's ever raised the issue before. Certainly, when we faced this challenge, we took the approach that we should grin and bear it rather than try and change it. That worked for us. But speaking up and bringing a new perspective to the process may enhance the outing for everyone. The idea that some may feel uncomfortable with the activity may not be widely understood.

Also, reach out to other novices. It's likely you're not the only one trying the activity for the first time. Mitzi experienced her first hunting expedition with two other women on her team, "That helped make it less stressful. We were all in—together."

You can also try some tricks to mitigate the potential problems. Says Lori:

> I employ a strategy that was taught to me by my husband from when he was a consultant and quickly realized it was better to remain sober during client dinners, but not draw

attention to himself by "not drinking." I order a vodka soda on the rocks with lime. It's a clear drink and as the ice melts, it looks like the drink is still full. Then, no one bothers me to order another, and I can remain sober while still being social. Sometimes I'll signal to the waiter (when they're at the table refilling water glasses) to fill up my glass. No one notices and it allows me to nurse one clear-liquid drink all evening.

If you're the boss . . .

Recognize that not everyone finds sports or fishing or Hooters fun. Whatever company traditions may be, look for ways that outings can be inclusive. Diversify the planning committees for outings so that all voices are heard. Ask for suggestions from staffers for events they'd like to try. Get feedback afterwards to see if there are ways the outing can be tweaked or enhanced. Don't be afraid to plan activities that might skew female. "Can you think of any times where they picked a traditionally female activity and then asked the men to flex to it?" asks Lori. To do so would be a statement from the boss that everyone can expand their horizons a bit on this subject, she says.

The new idea may be welcome by all, says Dawn.

When I worked at Parthenon, a consulting firm with many women at the earlier levels, they asked the associates what they wanted to do at the company party. The result was a highly inclusive set of options for all and one mandatory group cooking class. Events were fun, dress-up, competitive events. Everyone had fun at all the events and everyone found something they wanted to do. I was surprised by the number of guys that did not choose golf but instead hiking or biking or the cooking classes. So, bosses, think about planning new and inclusive events that surprise and offer something for everyone. And make the group activities unisex. This, from an avid golfer.

Lori argues for gender-neutral fun events.

There are many, *many* activities that are gender-neutral. Cooking classes. Scavenger hunts. Bowling. Karaoke. Puzzles/ brain busters. Charades. When I worked in Pepsi Foodservice, I also organized many trend tours in different cities to explore different food/beverage/retail trends. When I was at Keurig, teams bonded over charitable activities such as cleaning up a river front or serving food at a soup kitchen together.

An additional step for leaders: schedule more than one event— and then make sure you participate in the one that might perhaps be called non-traditional. So, if the day's events include golf and cooking—you pick the cooking. If it's hunting and hiking, you go on the hike. Do this even if your preferred activity might be horseback riding three hours to go fly fishing. When you participate in the "alternate" activity, you give it the seal of approval. It will then be seen as equal to other events scheduled.

Remember that offsite events you plan are not just for internal bonding. They also serve as recruiting tools. What do your offsites say about the type of people you want to attract? Do your events broadcast a willingness to embrace new ideas and a broad range of cultures? Or does your offsite telegraph a reverence for the past? Look at company outings as a way to have fun but also represent your brand.

If you're the witness . . .

If you're having fun, great. Are the people around you having fun, too? Be aware of your surroundings and the impact the fun may be having on all the participants. Also, add your voice when a suggestion for a new or different outing is raised. Support the idea of inclusive outings, even if you like deep sea fishing just fine.

Also, you can reach out to teach someone. Lori recalls this helped her:

> Early on in my career I worked for a VP and SVP who were both avid golfers. It was in the glory days of Pepsi when we were making lots of money as a company, and off-site meetings were plentiful. We often went to amazing locations for department meetings that involved playing golf at world-famous resorts. After one off-site meeting at Pinehurst Resort where others played golf while I sat in my room and returned phone calls (with my DayTimer because it was the 90s!), my boss took me aside and said, "I'm going to teach you the basics of golf. You're a high potential future executive and you're not going to get anywhere sitting in your room alone while the men bond over golf." The following Friday afternoon, we spent our "summer hours" together on a public golf course near our office. She wasn't a pro so she couldn't teach me a great golf swing in three hours, but she showed me all the things you need to know when actually *playing* golf—where to stand when someone is teeing off, where to park your cart, how to traverse the fairway in perfect right angles, how to walk on a green without messing up someone else's putt, how to pull up the flag for someone when they're putting, what to do when

your ball goes in the water, how to hit a ball out of the bunker, how to rake the sand, etc. For the non-golfers, this might sound like utter gibberish, but the golfers reading this will understand that it takes years to perfect your golf swing, but if you know the basics of golf etiquette, you can at least play in a scramble. To be clear, I'm a terrible golfer, and 90 percent of the golf I've played was at PepsiCo customer outings, but I always felt comfortable playing in a charity tournament or a scramble format because I knew my way around the course and I didn't slow down the game for others or do things (other than hit very poorly!) that would make others roll their eyes. Note to the reader: this session with my boss happened in 1990 and I still remember it like it was yesterday. Three hours out of her life allowed me to much more easily fit into a culture where golf was a big part of customer entertaining!

CHAPTER 20

Oh, *You're* in Our Foursome?

How to handle when you know you're not welcome

There's a moment at which a barrier is lowered, but all is not really resolved.

Women face this frequently in the workplace. The official barriers have fallen. Women can hold all manner of professional positions.

They are in the office, in the conference rooms, in the labs. But while they are physically included, they often find there's yet another set of challenges ahead. This happens when they step into a new situation and look at the faces around them that telegraph clearly: you're not supposed to be here.

We've experienced this phenomenon and we've given it a name: the inauthentic invite. It's the experience of being granted access to the party but feeling the vibe that says you're not really wanted.

It's not as amorphous as it sounds. Indeed, when you experience the inauthentic invite, it's vividly clear.

Here's Cie's story:

> I was set to play Pebble Beach Golf resort where one head-quarters person was going to be assigned to join three of our distributor partners in a golf scramble. These distributors were all men who worked together, played golf together, and knew each other very well.
>
> I will always remember the feeling as I walked up to meet my new teammates. As I approached the first tee, I could tell by their body language they were pissed that they were going to be playing with a woman.
>
> I was already nervous enough with my rusty golf skills but their reaction made everything worse. At that moment I regretted that I had volunteered to play and was thinking this was going to be a long and painful afternoon.
>
> As we were getting ready to start, they were all laughing and chumming it up together on the men's tee box. They all hit the ball far, but none landed in our fairway. We drove our carts down to the women's tee and as I approached the tee box

alone in absolute silence, I could feel my new teammates quietly watching me.

Imagine this story depicted as a comic strip. What would the thought bubbles above Cie's teammates say? Do you imagine they read: *"Welcome, Cie!"* No. When the inauthentic invite emerges, it's really not that hard to spot.

If the story of Cie's tense tee-off feels at all familiar, it's probably because you had some version of the experience growing up. Hiring and employee assessment firm Prevue says that kind of cold shoulder is really nothing more than adult cliques. "They are established based on conventional stereotypes rooted in assumptions and prejudice. Although many companies these days have made it their new mission to engage in diversity and inclusion, 43 percent of employees say cliques are still present at the office." And that, Prevue goes on to say, is evidence of a failed diversity and inclusion strategy.

Indeed, while the inauthentic invite may seem like a small slight, experts say it should act as a canary in a coal mine—a sign that inclusion is not taking hold.

Workplace exclusion—even a perceived sense of not belonging—can have an impact on a business. A study led by researchers at the University of Ottawa found that those who are ostracized at work are more likely to leave the organization than even those who have been harassed. Being ignored, the researchers say, is more discomforting than being engaged in a verbal dispute. It's considered more mundane than harassment, they said, but it is far more prevalent and can be connected more frequently to actual turnover within an organization.

Interestingly, a study by researchers at the University of Northern Iowa found men were more negatively affected than women when experiencing what they termed "perceived exclusion in the workplace." Men, they said, derive more of their self-esteem from work than women. And women, they posit, may have had more experience dealing with peer aggression as adolescents. (Thanks, high school?)

But if a cafeteria full of Mean Girls prepared us, we learned in the corporate workplace not to let an inauthentic invite stop us from advancing professionally.

Here's how Cie's story turned out:

> I was very nervous—I needed to get my ball in the fairway or at least in play. I ended up having a surprisingly clean drive. By the third hole my new teammates figured out there was actually a huge advantage to have me on the team as the women's tees at Pebble are significantly closer to the greens. It certainly was more comfortable that I was useful to the team, but I think the afternoon and connections would have been the same regardless of my level of play.
>
> Many important relationships are built in informal settings outside of the office. Women in general are involved in fewer of these events and not as likely to be included, or less likely to join in some of the extracurricular activities like golf, pick-up basketball or drinking. That afternoon I made connections and started new business relationships that I would not have developed had I not put myself out there and played in the scramble.

Angelique still has the "trophy" from her triumph over the inauthentic invite:

I had nearly the same situation as Cie. I was twenty years old, first job out of school, and I signed up for the golf outing as a new analyst in Merrill Lynch Investment Banking. I had never played golf before, but I assumed this was just a fun way for me to get to know my colleagues. I had no idea that everyone else already knew how to play.

At the start of the outing, I realized that I was put in the foursome that included the head of the department. I was a little intimidated, so I asked my direct manager for tips. I told him, "By the way, I've never played golf before." I still remember his face—it was as if I just told him I made a huge mistake in a buyout model that changed all the numbers. He was beside himself. He said I was going to ruin the department head's day! I had no idea it was that big a deal—isn't it just a game? I was so naive! So, he quickly gave me a few tips on how to swing the golf club at the tee, and since it was a game of best ball, maybe it wouldn't be a complete disaster.

Two surprising things happened: One—it turns out my years of playing mini-golf made me quite good on the green, and the foursome was thrilled to use my ball several times.

Two—under the best ball rules, the foursome has to use everyone's drive at least once. All I needed was one good drive and the team would be fine. Turns out, my colleagues were more than happy to give me tips and were thrilled to see their coaching turn into progress. When I got the one good drive we needed, they all shared in my success!

Our team did very well, and the head of the department was so pleased to tell the story at the party afterwards of how he coached this never-played-before newbie to create our team's success. He awarded me with the "most improved" award for the tournament, and my prize of a Merrill Lynch umbrella is still in my closet, carrying those fond memories.

When Mitzi approached her inauthentic invite, she had no illusions:

I'm in the "glass is half-full" camp, which is to say an unauthentic invite is better than no invite at all. I learned, over time, that it was best not to labor over the "late invite" or lack of authenticity in the invite, but to focus on the opportunity the invite provided. What could I learn, what relationship could I forge or strengthen, what new insight could I gain? And yes, I did think about how to make my presence felt, in a positive way, so that the next invitations would be authentic, and early.

I played basketball in college and enjoyed joining the basketball games that were frequently the team outings during Team Staff Meetings. I remember moving to the West Coast and being asked if I wanted to play basketball during similar meetings. Since I was new to this team, and the only female direct report to the GM, I was not sure whether the invite was authentic or not—but I accepted the invitation. Judging from the trash talking that quickly ensued, they didn't know that I could play ball. Half-way through our play, I was guarding one of the GMs and I blocked his shot—this was all the basketball credibility I needed. That blocked shot, and my ability to play, to show up to play with the team, enabled us to connect and engage faster and on a deeper level than would have been the case had I not accepted the invitation. The connections transferred quickly to jump start and enhance our working relationships.

Our Gen Z and millennial colleagues say the inauthentic invite is alive and well in today's workplaces. There are times, said one, when you are being included but you know it's out of obligation. Not because your male co-workers like your company. Another young woman described a Trivia Night, a weekly tournament at the bar near the office. Her department fielded a team. "When a male team member walks in, they all shout his name in greeting. When a female team member walks in, there's no such reception." We're allowed to be there, she says, but that's about it.

How can you tackle the inauthentic invite?

If it's you . . .

We're agreed on this topic. No matter how weak the invitation may seem, hold your head high and do it. Says Dawn:

> Invitations offered, however strained, are offered because they feel they should invite you. Take that to mean you should go because it has value in their mind. I was asked by an all-male group of Pepsi distributors once to go to Scotland and play a few rounds with their group. I would pay my own way of course. I felt that some really thought it would be nice to have me, and others not so sure. I went, and played the betting games, and won. Immediately I was more respected and ended up having a great time and forging personal relationships that helped in business as well.

Another time I can remember a sales associate describing to me being asked by Pepsi distributors to go on a wild pig hunt with them in Texas. This made my Scottish golf trip seem like a piece of cake! To her credit she went, learned a ton, was scared in the trees, but lived to tell the tales and earned many, many brownie points for going. Turns out they really wanted her to come but thought she would say no or be offended and hence the weak invitation. An invitation is an invitation. Go if you can and make the most of it. It may reap more rewards than working four weekends in a row in the office.

What's more, says Katie, particularly when it comes to a sports situation, don't overthink it:

I took golf lessons when I was in my mid-twenties so that I could participate in what I assumed would be an important part of my career. I am a decidedly average golfer but what I learned early on is that so are most men. Being comfortable not being an expert is something that most men seem to have mastered. Women, on the other hand, in general are given less permission and are more likely to hold themselves to higher standards. I think that even if the invitation was offered begrudgingly, it's a good rule of thumb to go along and make the most of it. Chances are you are not going to be the worst person at whatever the activity is. And even if you are, then you are making a lot of people happy by saving them from that fate.

If you're the boss . . .

Treat ostracism the same way you treat harassment—and come

down hard when you see it. Organizations must educate managers about the nature and consequences of ostracizing workers and implement policies that define and discourage exclusion. Managing relationship tensions should be part of the discussion around workplace behavior.

As a boss, you can anticipate who might feel awkward at an outing. Ask someone on your team to take that person under their wing, or better yet, include that person in your group. It will speak volumes to other leaders about the need to be inclusive.

Also, consider putting your money where your mouth is.

If you're the witness . . .

Imagine Cie's Pebble Beach experience one more time. Now picture one of the three men stepping forward to shake her hand as she walked up. The difference between "Oh, are you in our foursome?" and "Welcome to our foursome!" can't be understated. If you're the witness to the exclusion, it may take only the smallest effort on your part to dispel it. When you see exclusion, counter it with inclusion.

CHAPTER 21

Office Chatter

How workplace gossip can be good—and bad

L et's talk about office chatter.

Casual conversation around the office can be a great benefit. It can give you the inside scoop on coming change. It can help you navigate tricky relationships. It can help you read between the lines of official information and figure out your best way forward.

It can also have a downside. When casual conversation is mean-spirited or designed to damage another person, it is a corrosive force. Nasty gossip, when it gets out of hand, can get out of the building and into the larger conversation around your industry. There's no upside when your competition finds out you're a house divided, with internal sniping a common occurrence in your halls.

So, this chapter is about gossip—the good kind and the bad kind. And how to make sure you know the difference—and the impact.

The word gossip comes with a host of negative connotations, most of which are heaped on women. It's unusual to hear a man referred to as a gossip, but it's a label women get all the time. When we say gossip, we don't mean idle, nasty comments. The good kind of gossip might even benefit from its alternate name—watercooler chatter. The advent of remote work and personal water bottles might make that water cooler image outdated, but the distinction is important.

Some idle conversations around the workplace are beneficial. Others are not.

But whatever our opinion or name for it, office gossip happens. Researchers at the University of Amsterdam suggest that a whopping 90 percent of total office conversation qualifies as gossip. A study from the Georgia Institute of Technology found gossip makes up 15 percent of all office email. Whether we like it or not, gossip is present in the office and a routine factor in our conversations.

What's more, gossip is an activity that society views as largely female. In an article for *Forbes* magazine, research psychologist Dr. Peggy Drexler points out that men and women talk about each other in the workplace but "what is called gossip for women, for men is just shooting the breeze."

Gossip factors into our experiences as women in the workplace. How we handle it can impact how we are perceived and our relationships with co-workers.

Research suggests not all office gossip is bad. A study led by researchers at the University of Baltimore acknowledges a long list of upsides: office gossip enforces group norms, allows for indirect social comparisons, increases the intimacy of social bonds, communicates information, clarifies group membership, and enhances perceptions of status and power. Indeed, in an office setting, gossip is often an invaluable source of information for newcomers. The company handbook may tell you the rules and regulations, but it's watercooler gossip that will help you find your way in the maze of interpersonal relationships that make up a corporate setting. Who gets along with whom? Who is considered prickly? Supportive? Dangerous? How do you "read between the lines" of the boss's memos? This is the critical information that everyone needs and nobody writes down. You'll hear it in the hallways and the break rooms. When viewed from the recipient's perspective, gossip clearly has value.

But the science on gossip is hardly clear. While some studies may cast it as women making a power move, others may paint a different picture. Says Angelique: "I can think of women I've worked with who were known as gossipers. They were seen as connectors and culture builders—people in the know, with their finger on the pulse of the firm."

Drexler points out that while some workplaces have tried to limit gossip or create "no gossip" zones, the results are clear: it doesn't work. Wherever there are groups of people, there will be gossip, she says. It's part of human nature.

We've seen the good and the bad.

Says Katie:

I think workplace gossip of the right kind can be incredibly helpful. When I was in one of my first jobs after business school, I distinctly remember many occasions sitting around "gossiping"—but it was always about the business and the power dynamics. It was a true "shoot the shit" situation where we would talk about what happened behind the scenes from a big meeting that happened recently, who was on the ins or outs, what we would do if we were in charge, etc. We talked about the business from a higher level than our low-level jobs and I think it made me a much more aware employee who could advocate for myself better and position myself better because I understood the dynamics better.

COVID helped one of our younger colleagues see the upside of gossip.

One young rising star with a track record of success was recruited into her dream job just as all work was going fully remote due to COVID restrictions. She had always prided herself in being able to navigate office politics smoothly and get along with colleagues well and felt this skill set was instrumental in her success. But, sitting in her makeshift home office interacting with faces in boxes on Zoom all day, she found herself feeling completely rudderless.

> I was lost. I couldn't get any traction on projects and I realized how much I was missing by not being there. It took me weeks to realize that two of my co-workers really dislike each other. It would have taken me all of ten minutes sitting in a room with them or one passing comment from a friend in the office. If I had been in the office talking with people, I could have avoided wasting so much time.

How to handle gossip:

If it's you . . .

Keep chatter verbal. Putting anything in writing, even if innocent or positively intended, could backfire. Says Cie:

> One of my first bosses told me to be very careful about what I write in emails. He said assume anything you write will be re-printed on the front page of the *Wall Street Journal*— and if I would not be comfortable with it showing on the front page, don't hit send. I never forgot that piece of advice. To this day I think about anything I write through that lens.

Extend that rule to all devices: email, Slack, Yammer, text, Zoom. Remember that the chat feature in Zoom is not private and remember that anything you put in writing can be screen-grabbed and saved.

Furthermore, ask yourself: Why am I saying this? What is my motivation? Watercooler chatter runs like a laugh track through our office lives, but we can monitor our own reasons for engaging. But don't shrug it off entirely. Chatter can be very informative. Says Katie: "If you are not gossiping with your fellow employees, you are most likely out of the loop."

If you're the boss . . .

Use gossip as a metric. It's a measure of how well your company is functioning. Says Angelique:

> A company that invests a lot of effort in promoting certain principles or values should see those in action in the casual settings where behavior is harder to enforce. If there is a lot of consistency at the top in acting by those principles, I would assume it would also be seen in the casual settings. If there is a big say-do gap, then it would be very visible in office gossip.

If you're the witness . . .

Watch out for a double standard.

> Cie remembers some crazy holiday parties where there were always hysterical stories that would be shared around the office the next day. There were always several people who were overserved and that led to wild dancing, aggressive flirting, and/or someone getting sick. The behavior would be identical

for both the men and women but postmortem stories were clearly not similar. The watercooler talk was all: "Did you see how drunk Julia got? I saw Julia kissing some guy in accounting." Very rarely was a male gossiped about for even more questionable behavior—that fell under the category of *"boys will be boys."*

Add your voice to end that double standard.

Section Five

Hiring and Promotions

Perhaps the most damaging of everyday indignities takes place in the hiring and promotion process. These are the interactions that cost women money, promotions, and careers. We have been on all sides of this process. We have been young women, eager to move up. We have been at mid-career, jockeying for a place in the leadership ranks. And we have been senior leaders, working at the highest level of our companies. We have seen the hiring and promoting process up close and personal. This is what we've learned.

CHAPTER 22

He's a Great Guy

How boys' club language influences careers

Let's talk about the "boys' club."

It's a phenomenon well-discussed in business circles. The "boys' club" or "old boys' network" is the legendary construct that allows white men to advance while women and people of color are shut out of the plum positions. In generations past, the clubs were physical spaces—colleges, university clubs, smoking clubs, golf courses—that restricted membership to white men and functioned as exclusive platforms for them to conduct business.

Today, most (not all) clubs have dropped their restrictions. But the system that advanced men remains. You may not be able to see it, but if you listen, you can hear it. The boys' club functions today in the language men use to help each other move up in the world.

Katie was in a new leadership position when it clicked for her.

I remember sitting in at a performance review meeting with my peers, my boss, and HR. It may have been the first time they had done a talent planning session where each function head reported key accomplishments and development opportunities for their team. Our HR person was happy to have me there since she knew I understood the process. As we went around the room, I'll never forget how many times it seemed that the key assessment point for a man being discussed was literally: "He's a good guy."

The use of "good guy" matters. It's the shorthand for: He's one of us. In other words, he's a member of the club.

Who needs a physical clubhouse when you can get a wave up the corporate ladder like that?

When it comes to hiring and promotion, the boys' network remains a major force. Even when companies make efforts at diversity, the impact of male friendship and preference remains in place. A female candidate may need to jump through hoop after hoop to be considered while a male candidate's resume is advanced when one buddy on the inside says, "I know a great guy." A woman on the inside, in search of a promotion, may find the spot goes to a man whom colleagues describe as "a good guy" with "good presence." Breaking this pattern is especially challenging since so much of the good will is generated through social gatherings that routinely lack women, such as sports leagues. Angelique once counseled a young woman who spoke with her after seeking advice on advancement from a senior man. This man had let the young woman in on his secret to success.

His secret to getting his ideas heard was time invested on weekends running with the boss and a group of other men. Yes, they were all men. He did not seem to notice that his tip was not actually an accessible approach for the junior woman. She left the discussion feeling like she had no way to break into this club and did not have a path to gain that critical benefit of the doubt that comes from the trust of social bonding.

The club system is alive and well in the halls of corporate America. Researchers Zoe Cullen and Ricardo-Perez Truglia teamed up in 2020 to produce the study titled "The Old Boys' Club: Schmoozing and the Gender Gap." They found men assigned to male managers were promoted faster than men assigned to female managers—and all women regardless of managers' gender. Physical proximity made the difference. Men who took breaks with their managers were more likely to reap professional benefits. To test this concept more intensely, the researchers carved out a specific scenario, analyzing the advancement of men in a particular financial firm who smoked. When male employees who smoked worked for male managers who smoked, they took smoke breaks with their managers and were subsequently promoted at higher rates than those who worked for non-smokers. "According to the schmoozing channel, that increase in social interactions will translate into higher promotion rates," they wrote. And with promotions come raises. The study concluded more than one-third of the pay gap between men and women can be traced back to this informal social connection—the knowledge that the other fellow is a "great guy."

Once we learned to look for it, the experience of the "great guys" around us was quite obvious.

Says Cie:

I remember hearing "Tim is a great guy" as an endorsement when we had to figure out who we were going to promote into a newly vacated senior manager position. I came to find out that Tim was known primarily from a pick-up basketball game. Once I was sensitized to the "Tim is a good guy" dynamic I noticed if it was not a pick-up basketball connection—it was a connection from a golf outing or grabbing beers after work, but it was not uncommon for the connection to be totally unrelated to work performance in the office. Or even more removed, someone heard that "Tim was a great guy" from his friends who play in his basketball league.

When an individual is known and liked by other people and they hang out socially it is easier for them to support, recommend, and take chances on that individual. No doubt this dynamic happens among both men and women. The critical difference is that men are in the key leadership positions in much higher numbers—so when knowing of, or hearing that someone is a "good guy," it puts women at a disadvantage.

Angelique's experience with the old boys' club concept prompted her realization that it didn't just hurt women—it created a hurdle for the business.

I recall a long time ago when we were interviewing candidates that we talked about "the airplane test." The idea was that you would enjoy sitting on a long airplane flight with this person, as a measure of "cultural fit." A version of the "good guy" filter. It made sense to me at the time, because you want an office environment where people like each other.

It is only in hindsight that I realize how much bias that brings into the process. I will likely enjoy talking to people I already have a lot in common with. How does that encourage real diversity of thought? And shouldn't it be more important to respect each other than like each other?

I remember interviewing a man for a position on my team. His resume said he had worked for years on a feminine products line. I asked about that—how did that exactly work? How could he understand what his audience needed without any personal experience? He said, "I'm a really good listener." Indeed, he was! And a great hire too. I think of it often in recruiting to find the right mindset—not necessarily the people who think like us and know what we know. Instead of looking for "cultural fit," we should look for a "cultural add."

We asked our younger colleagues to reflect on the old boys' network and its influence today. Here's what they said:

> Men are more comfortable with men. So, they're going to stretch Bill into the role, bring Bill along, take Bill to lunch, coach him. We like talking with Bill, we're comfortable with Bill—we know we'll be able to call Bill on Friday at 7 p.m. We don't really know Lia. We don't know what she likes. We're not as comfortable. Can we call Lia on a Friday at 7 p.m.? So, they don't stretch women into roles as well or take them under their wings.

How should you handle the presence—and power—of the boys' club?

If it's you . . .

Find ways to connect and build relationships with those who are hiring managers and/or are participating in promotion decisions. Says Mitzi:

Women and people of color need more people in the room that know us and our work, and will say, "Veronica is a great woman!" Very early in my career, I thought if you did great work, the rest would take care of itself. I learned quickly, you have to do great work, people have to know about the work you are doing, and leaders need to feel comfortable working with you.

Adds Cie:

The idea of thinking that all you need to do is put your head down, do great work and the rest will take care of itself is alive and well for women. This is due to the fact that we have a sixteen-year educational track record reinforcing that belief. In school if you studied, attended, and paid attention in lectures and turned in homework assignments you could get very good grades. And your grade in class or your SAT score was not negatively influenced by the popular guy that did not take school as seriously. You would get an A and Mr. Popular would get a B. But in the workplace that dynamic can totally shift—it is not enough to be a diligent employee. Relationships and connections play a huge role in success.

Angelique adds:

This is a very important lesson to emphasize, and learn early. Self-promotion is not just good for you—it is good for the teams you manage. And prioritizing the investment of time to find someone who will be a sponsor takes effort, but it needs to be made clear to women that it is not a "nice thing to do." At the higher levels which tend to rely on more of an emotional response, those sponsors are make-or-break.

If you're the boss . . .

Recognize the system as penalizing for women—even when not everyone else can see it. Says Lori:

> Sometimes the Good Guy thing means we are actually holding women to higher standards. Recently one of my corporate boards was looking to add an additional board member. I had spoken up strongly that we needed to add another woman to the board. My fellow board members agreed—with the caveat that "the fit had to be right." When we had our conference call to review the candidates (three men and three women), I noticed a disturbing pattern. With the woman candidates, our most senior board director asked the recruiter to explain *why* the woman had made each of her transitions. Was she fired from XYZ company, or did she leave voluntarily? We did not ask these questions for the three male candidates.
>
> In the spirit of assuming positive intent and realizing that a great deal of bias is unconscious, I counted to ten and calmly said: "Jim [not his real name!], I'm sure this is not intentional, but we have only asked the recruiter to investigate the reasons behind transition for the female candidates. I know you meant no ill intent here, but let's resolve either to ask the question for all the candidates or not ask it at all." Before I could get the words out of my mouth, a fellow director texted me and

said, "That was the most helpful comment a board member has ever made."

What is the lesson? No one had any ill intent, but you have to use your seat at the table to speak up and bring the conversation back to competencies, skills, and process. There are times when humor might be a helpful tool, but in these cases I think you can elevate the conversation without attacking your peers or even poking fun at them.

Stick up for women. Says Mitzi: "As leaders, we have to make sure we are advocating for talented female leaders the way our male counterparts advocate for men. I sometimes think women set a higher bar for other women."

If you're the witness . . .

Finally, when "he's a great guy" drifts into the conversation, point it out as off topic. Chances are, most will see that and agree. Says Lori:

> I've often heard my male colleagues start off by describing a male employee as a good guy. I have found it very easy to say, "I'm glad Employee X is likable; that's always helpful. Can you please elaborate on where he is on the sales competency model and what you've seen in the past year about his ability to influence, lead, bring others with him, create challenging plans and execute with excellence?" It doesn't need to be snitty in any way; you just bring the conversation back to competency.

CHAPTER 23

She's Too Emotional

Dealing with emotions in the workplace

"Crying at the office will kill a woman's career."

Raise your hand if you've heard that one.

Women are often counseled on the art of showing emotions at work. Research shows women can be more effective leaders than men because they do use emotion and are empathetic. Their emotions can bring strengths to the corporate culture. And yet, when it comes to individual women, the advice is often less positive in tone.

A woman must be tough, but not off-putting. Passionate but not angry. Strong but not cold. Nurturing but not soft. Likable but not a doormat. A woman must never show anger, fear, or sadness. She also must not appear timid, cold, or risk-averse. If all of that sounds like a contradictory emotional mess, it is. Women often find it hard to navigate the rules around showing emotion because when it comes to women at work, the norms are fluid. One day, a woman will be told she needs to be tough, aggressive, willing to duke it out with the guys. Another, a woman will be criticized for being too emotional, too angry, too out-of-control.

To be sure, the office is no place for emotional theatrics. But when emotions are expressed, women tend to attract more scrutiny and criticism. Jacqueline S. Smith of the University of Massachusetts joined forces with Victoria L. Brescoll of Yale and Erin L. Thomas, an HR diversity specialist to write about the topic. In their book, *Handbook on Well-Being of Working Women*, they point out the contradiction women battle every day around emotions at work. Women are penalized for showing masculine-type emotions such as anger and aggression. They're also criticized for showing more female emotions, such as sadness, and are judged as lacking emotional control. Gender stereotypes constrain the way women experience emotion at work by granting them a much narrower range of acceptable behavior. Men, on the other hand, can express more emotions without backlash.

And don't bother trying to repress emotion to navigate the workplace. A cool, detached persona will likely get you labeled with the "B" word in a hurry.

Particularly in leadership roles, women may find a display of emotion—of any kind—will draw critics. The coverage of Hilary Clinton's first run for president, in which she battled Barack Obama for the nomination is a good case study for this phenomenon. At a campaign event in New Hampshire, Clinton choked up while answering a question about how she maintained her passion and drive. "It's not easy, and I couldn't do it if I didn't passionately believe it was the right thing to do," said Clinton, in what ABC News reported as "getting visibly emotional."

The news story then delivered a parade of experts criticizing Clinton's display of emotion. Words like "outburst" were used to describe her delivery. One expert acknowledged that Candidate Clinton faced a unique problem: she had to appear strong and tough but not shrill and bitchy. The expert had no advice on how Clinton might walk that emotional tightrope.

Indeed, we are all still looking for the right response to the emotions question.

Mitzi drew her guidelines from sports.

One of my basketball coaches used to say, "don't celebrate too much after a win and don't pout too much after a loss," advocating for a more balanced emotional response. This seemed to stick with me and informed my leadership style. People expect leaders to be consistent and level-headed. Move too far out of the "level-headed" emotional range and you risk being labelled a wide variety of things. I found it better to respond rather than react—that is to think about the impact of your behavior, how your behavior will best be received versus an automatic, knee-jerk reaction. It's also helpful to be aware of what and who triggers emotions for you.

On the other hand, attempting to be emotionless at work is not beneficial, Mitzi says. "People need to know how we feel about things and situations. We don't need to overthink things to the point where we stop speaking up or speaking out. We just need to always be mindful of how we express ourselves."

That said, many of us struggled to find the best way to keep our emotions from interfering with our careers. Says Katie:

> This has always been a challenge for me. I'm generally quick to show emotion and, as Cie knows, I do not have a good poker face. I once jokingly asked HR if they would pay for my Botox so that I would have a more frozen face in meetings. They declined.
>
> I think women absolutely have a narrower range of acceptable emotions in the workplace than men do. But I think showing humanity and a genuine human reaction also makes people more relatable, so shutting down all emotion is not always helpful either. I have tried to practice counting to ten, take a deep breath, go for a walk, press my fingernails into my palm, etc., and have not always been successful. This can be such a personal thing. But your reaction does need to be calibrated and appropriate for the situation. If that seems impossible, taking a moment (or an hour) to gather yourself is far better than an overly passionate reaction in the moment. The more senior you are, you can't be an unpredictable hothead.

To be fair, men also face criticism for showing emotion at work—at least some emotions. Crying at work, for example, generates more of a negative for men than it does for women, reports a study published in the European *Journal of Social Psychology*. A crying man is perceived as more emotional and less competent than a crying woman, the study found.

But when it comes to the full spectrum of emotions, the process is more complicated for women. Our colleagues—peers and rising leaders alike—tell us they wrestle with the conflicting signals around emotions at work.

"I feel like I got a lot of 'you're being emotional' feedback when I was passionate or committed to something," said one colleague. "I don't think a man in my position would have gotten that. To a man, they'd say: "Oh, he's so strong. He's so powerful He owns his shit, and he isn't afraid of conflict." But I was seen as emotional."

One rising leader told us this story. "One of my very best friends worked with a manager who was quite emotional himself. You would see his anger, but that wouldn't really be called emotional—for men, it's passionate. But this manager, he would poke at her soft spots, gaslight her. And then when she reacted, tell her she was too emotional."

The confusion around women's emotions likely stems from far more complex and ingrained cultural issues than we can untangle here. So, we will stick to the practical. Our emotions are a part of us. How can we handle the emotional quicksand at work?

If it's you . . .

Because there are so many mixed signals around the issue of emotionality, many of us have simply developed our own set of tactics over years of trial and error. The only thing we agree on is that there is no single right answer for women.

Here's Lori's take: "I have been in so many situations at work where I just wanted to cry. I don't mean sad tears like when I found out a colleague had died, but the kind of angry tears where my level of frustration was at its peak or when I felt like I was being unfairly criticized or was being passed over for a big promotion." Her advice?

> When I'm in a situation where I feel tears coming on or I'm so angry that I can't speak, I just start taking notes. I'm not sure if it's so that I can put a little space in while I get my composure, or whether it's actually that writing things down helps me process the many thoughts swirling around in my head. Either way, it buys me some time to gain my composure and frame my thoughts. Usually by looking down at my pad of paper, I can gain enough composure to say something like, "I'd like to take a few minutes to think about this conversation. If it's okay, I'm going to grab a cold glass of water, and I'll be back to finish the conversation." Remember, oftentimes when women are at the point of tears, it's because of anger—and that is a different way than most men express anger. Try to understand *what* it was that made you so angry. Don't worry about the fact that you may have cried; bring the conversation back to the underlying issue.

Dawn takes a slightly different view of emotions at work. They're real, she says. When displayed at the strategically right time, they can work for you.

> Emotion is a natural part of life. How you show emotion is part of what makes you you. But emotion in a business environment needs to be saved for moments that matter and not every day. I think men and women would approach this

similarly, although women may get pegged as being more emotional, which is biased of course. But if one is emotional on a regular basis at work, it may interfere with people taking you seriously. I like to be as even-keeled as I can be and try to verbalize when I think things are wrong or great and why. When I do feel very strongly, emotional, about something, I think it stands out and people notice because I do not wear my emotions on my sleeve all the time. I think men tend to be better than women at restraint and they use an explosion of emotion to make a point and often change the perspective of the room. So, I advise that yes, try to be yourself, but pause and think before speaking to make sure that your anger or over-the-top passion is best used for those situations.

If you're the boss . . .

Says Mitzi:

Consider how you might foster an environment where there is less judgment around emotions as "good" or "bad." Emotions provide information. In any given situation, I believe people use facts to determine what should be done. How people feel and what's important to them informs what will get done and how it will get done. If you want a complete picture, seek to understand not just the facts, but how individuals feel about a situation and why things are important to them—what they value.

Don't forget, you're the boss, not a girlfriend. Says Katie:

> I have had times when people came to me with what was
> fairly petty or trivial workplace drama. I remember thinking
> that if I were my boss (a very direct, no-nonsense guy), no
> one would bring this stuff to him. Whereas my nature is to try
> and solve problems or hear people out, I had to catch myself
> in some of these cases and not let myself get pulled into the
> drama.

But ultimately, creating an emotional culture is part of your job.
The emotional landscape of a company is an important part of the
business's overall success. Offices have emotional cultures whether
you want them to or not. They're present even if they're not discussed.
With that in mind, leaders should see the creation and maintenance
of an emotional culture as part of their mandate. It can and should be
cultivated.

How can you create and lead a successful emotional culture?

Express the desire and ability to connect with emotions. You don't
want to foster a workplace of constant venting, but being open to hearing emotional issues is part of facing them and molding them into the
culture you desire. Let it be known that you will hear your team when
they express concerns or other emotion-laden issues.

Project the emotional culture you hope to create. The rest of the
office will take a cue from leadership and internalize the emotional
tenor as the appropriate, boss-approved attitude. If you want others to
act in a certain way, show that in your own behavior first.

Be flexible in your expectations. Whatever the desired emotional
culture, not everyone will feel that emotion every day. You may want

an emotional culture that is competitive or creative or nurturing. There will be days when it's not easy to connect to the desired emotional state, but let your team know you value that emotional culture, and that they should make the effort every day.

If you're the witness . . .

Call out the bias when you see it. Listen for the ways in which women's emotions are used against them.

Cie's colleague was contacted by a man who was interviewing a female candidate for a senior role and wanted to get her perspective around the candidate's "strong personality." He said he wanted to make sure her personality wouldn't be too strong for their culture.

After assuring him that the candidate had passion, smarts, and a strong track record, Cie's colleague pointed out to him that in her experience women get unduly scrutinized for having strong personalities while men get rewarded. She asked him: "Have you talked to her directly about your reservations?"

Calling this out undoubtedly made the male interviewer think twice about potential unfair stereotypes about women. A great example of being an ally and highlighting potential bias.

Also, observe how your workplace talks about emotions and sort in your own mind: is this a lopsided emotional culture? Is a man with a raised voice passionate but a woman with a raised voice angry? Are men given a pass for behavior that gets women tagged as "too emotional"? Say what you see. Raise the topic of emotional culture and how the standards may differ for men, women, and people of color. For example, says Mitzi, look at the coverage of the vice-presidential debate between Kamala Harris and Mike Pence. It's clear, she says, that Kamala Harris had to walk a fine line around expressing emotions in that setting. "Kamala had to be mindful of how she responded when Pence interrupted her and cut into her time."

The key, says Lori, is to approach the topic by asking questions.

> I think it is a way to get things that are unconscious to the surface without being overly critical or accusatory. When you think that we are unfairly criticizing women for being emotional, ask the question: Can you tell me how our culture deals with emotion? Do we want people to express anger, sadness, passion in an overt way or do we want people to stay "close to center" and not go high or low? Do you think there are any differences for men versus women? In getting an executive to talk aloud about the company, you can start to get at where there might be inconsistencies for men and women.
>
> I once said this in a meeting, and my colleague replied: "It's not so much how [the female executive] dealt with the situation we're talking about. It's more that it made us wonder how she would hold up when things got heated at a customer meeting or when a board member came down hard on her in a presentation." This was useful information for me; it helped me get to the real issue.

CHAPTER 24

Be Like Bill

How men take their self-worth all the way to the bank

A job posting goes live. Who will apply?

Men will apply for the job if they meet 60 percent of the stated requirements. Women, on the other hand, will only apply if they meet 100 percent of the requirements.

That stat, made famous by Sheryl Sandberg in her book *Lean In*, highlights a lurking threat to women's advancement into senior roles. Most of the time, we focus on the hurdles that are placed in front of us by others. But this is a hurdle we set up for ourselves: the voice in our head that talks us out of trying.

It's not that women go around muttering, "We're not worthy" under their breath. Instead, it's a matter of attitude.

The genesis of the *Lean In* data point turned out to be an internal report at a single company. But the underlying theme of women counting themselves out is one that turns up routinely in research and discussions of women's advancement. We've seen it. We've even lived it. Women are more inclined to hold back and wait to be noticed rather than make a play for a prized job or assignment. Meanwhile, our male counterparts go for it. Susan sees the job posting and thinks: if I acquire that one new skill, I'll be able to go for a job like this one. Bill sees the job posting and thinks: Why not me? I'm awesome!

It's time to be like Bill.

This chapter is about women leaning into their strengths and asking for what they want. It's about shrugging off conditioning that said women should be demure and understated. It's about bragging on what they've done rather than just focusing on what they could do better. As girls, so many of us were coached to put our heads down and work hard and wait to be noticed while the boys were taught to puff out their chests and boast.

Whatever lessons we learned on the schoolyard, it's time to recast that mindset for the office. Attitude is half the battle.

While the *Lean In* stat gets most of the press, there's plenty of research to back the phenomenon. LinkedIn drilled down into its job data and found that women apply for 20 percent fewer jobs than men. Indeed, women were 16 percent less likely than men to apply for a job after viewing it. "Women tend to screen themselves out of the conversation," the study found.

Many interpret this behavior as evidence that women lack self-confidence, and that's part of it. Leadership trainer Tara Mohr uncovered another reason: women were more likely to view the job description as "rules" and they were less inclined than men to break rules by applying.

Applying for jobs is just one sphere in which this mindset is problematic. When women fail to see themselves as qualified for a big job, they may also sell themselves short in other areas such as taking a plum assignment, asking for a raise, or seeking a promotion. The reluctance for self-promotion in all these areas creates a significant barrier to advancement—especially when Bill has no trouble at all tooting his own horn.

The issue runs deeper than just the workplace. Christine L. Exley and Judd B. Kessler, in their study for the National Bureau of Economic Research found that women tend to hold back in self-promotion even when they know their performance is equal to that of men. The gender gap in self-promotion is wide and extends as far back as middle school, their research showed. "It is difficult to mitigate," they noted.

We know. We've lived it.

Says Dawn: "My natural inclination was to so over-focus on committing to my own growth that I didn't toot my own horn."

Says Lori:

Anyone who has been in management roles for a long time can probably attest that, as a general rule, men and women approach career discussions and performance reviews differently. Men tend to come with great confidence about all the great things they've done the prior year and can lean heavily into why they think they are right for a raise, promotion, top performer review, etc. Women traditionally tend to focus on internalizing the constructive/development feedback and talk about all the things they want to work on in order to be 150 percent ready for the next role/promotion. Women will say they are ready for a role if they possess 90-plus percent of the qualities, while men will declare themselves ready with 40 percent of the qualifications.

I realized that I fell fully into this trap, and truthfully, found myself spending most of my time in performance reviews showing how well I understood the development feedback and talking about my plans to address in the upcoming year. Being humble and development-minded has its place, but when overused can position you for your current role and not necessarily for future/bigger roles.

Says Cie:

I remember the first time I got my first job out of business school. I was making $42,000 a year as an associate marketing manager—my previous job had been about $5/hour working at a bike shop—so I was thrilled. I remember telling my mom that I felt rich and if I never got a raise again the rest of my life but could maintain this salary, that would be amazing. Then, when I got promoted to assistant brand manager with a raise and was eligible for a bonus, I was over the moon. Not sure if it was my Midwestern upbringing, being female or what, but I approached the beginning of my career as pleasantly surprised with every promotion and raise. Quickly I noticed that my peers (who were mainly males) felt that their promotions were long overdue and the pay increases and bonuses were not quite what they expected.

Not sure my attitude or behavior ever changed much throughout my career. I was just lucky to work for good bosses and good companies that recognized and rewarded good performance. It is impossible to know if being more vocal about promotion timing and/or pay increases would have accelerated my career but I now know that I was in the minority not being more of an advocate for myself.

We asked our millennial and Gen Z colleagues about this topic. Here's what one told us:

> Men talk to men, they see where they are from a salary perspective. Women start at a lower salary and end up lower. And one reason we stay lower is because we're having conversations only with other women. For me, compared to my female friends, I was doing well. But I was not having the right conversations. I wasn't talking to any men, so I did not realize I was actually getting paid less than them. My barometer was off.

How can we catch Bill at his own game?

If it's you . . .
Says Mitzi:

> Ask for what you want! This was a game-changer for me. I was on the slate for a promotion to the next level, waiting for the right role to come available in our division. I was attending a meeting for the Pepsi Distributors and sat down to have a talk with a marketing colleague that I hadn't seen in a while. After our normal greeting, she said to me, "Our region is the only one with an open region VP role, you should be our region VP." My first thought was, "You're in a different division, I can't cross divisions." My second thought was, "You're absolutely right! I should be your RVP!" Fortunately, after a little discussion, I realized I had that twisted. My second thought should have been my first, and my first should have been my second. I sought out the division VP (hiring manager) at the meeting and let him know that I was very interested in his open region VP job and that I was definitely the right person for the role. He agreed and set all the next steps in motion. I got the job. Up to then, I had let the People Planning Processes play out; I had let opportunities come to me. From that point forward, I was much more proactive. I learned to "Be like Bill."

"Use your strengths to change the conversation," says Lori.

Once I realized the problem, I changed my approach. I used my towering strength (great organization skills and a psychotic need to prepare) to conquer the issue. I would come into every performance/career discussion with a list of things that I had accomplished and the rationale for why I was ready for the next role. I didn't rely on confidence or winging it, I relied on my strong preparation skills to give me the confidence and narrative to carry the discussion. I have a notoriously bad memory for facts and figures, so I had them ready in my notes in front of me fully prepared to share. I also had key bullet points on my notes, so that I could be concise and clear.

Says Cie:

The advice I give everyone is to be their own advocates and get comfortable talking about their accomplishments and have proactive career conversations. Ask for feedback and treat it as a gift. We all have areas that we can improve and if we do not hear constructive feedback, it is harder to improve. In fact, people will often assume that whatever they are doing is part of their success formula and will be resistant to change without some outside feedback. I loved hearing positive feedback but no doubt I grew more from constructive feedback.

If you're the boss . . .

Encourage women on your team to self-promote. Make it part of the feedback you give to ensure they improve in their jobs. Says Katie:

I once worked for a guy who was very receptive to scheduling breakfasts and lunches with employees from all over the company. I realized that it was usually the men showing up in a tie because they had scheduled lunch with him. I then realized that he always knew these guys by name and generally had a positive opinion of them but some of my best team members, not only women but more often than not, weren't on his radar because they weren't seeking out those opportunities. I began coaching the women that they should reach out and get on his calendar for a lunch or breakfast. Sometimes I had to explain how to do it; it had never occurred to them to be so forthright or they weren't sure what to talk about. I also focused on creating opportunities for women to showcase their projects or work in a more official setting. I would set up twenty-minute meetings for them to walk him through a project and get that valuable in-person time. I wanted to ensure that the women on my team had opportunities to be seen and to impress.

Also, police the review process to ensure that women are getting the credit they deserve and the Bills are not moving ahead based on bravado.

If you're the witness . . .

Amplify women. Notice and call out the good work of women on your team. Ensure that their achievements are discussed both officially, in promotion discussions, and casually, in office chatter. Including the work of women in these discussions raises the profile of their work and ensures that their efforts are noticed.

Be the power network for women. If you're in a senior role, make an effort to ensure the mentorship you offer works for both men and women. Track your engagement with more junior staffers and note the outcomes: Are men more likely to benefit than women from your mentorship? How can you make your help equally powerful?

CHAPTER 25

She's Not a Good Fit

How this vague line keeps women out of top positions

At a board meeting where Dawn was an independent director, a discussion took place around adding more members. The company wanted to add another woman to the male-dominated board. But the CEO had a caveat:

"She has to be the right fit."

Male nods all around. A woman, sure. But only if she's a good fit.

What is this "fit" that the men on the board valued so highly?

Fit is a word that seems so small, so casual. And yet it is a concept that will sink or save a woman applying for a position. Fit is a tiny word with a lot of power.

Fit is more than corporate speak. It is a concept rooted in science. The personality/job fit theory has been studied extensively by psychologists. The theory suggests that an individual's personality traits can predict success or failure within an organization. The better the match between individual and organization, the more effective that person will be on the job. Organizations began to use "fit" as a way to create a loyal, effective workforce. By matching the right personality with the right job, company workers can achieve a better synergy and avoid pitfalls such as high turnover and low job satisfaction. Employees are more likely to stay committed to organizations if the fit is "good."

But what started as a tool to ensure happy employees has morphed. The concept of fit has expanded to examine not simply whether an employee will embrace an organization, but whether the organization will embrace the employee. What was designed as a way to predict employee satisfaction now shifted to a filter for organizations to advance or deny certain individuals on the grounds that they would be a "bad" fit. This use of fit as a rejection criterion crops up routinely. It shows up in boardrooms, such as the one at which Dawn sat and the men around her pondered adding a woman, *maybe*. Fit, in its vagueness, has become a way to accept or reject someone without ever really saying why.

And this is where fit becomes fraught.

Companies want employees to be a good fit because that bolsters success, both for the employee and the organization. For that reason, leaders can't simply ban the use of fit as criteria. On the other hand, if fit is being used by an established majority to filter out newcomers who don't look, think, or act like them, then fit is a barrier to diversity and inclusion.

We have seen the fit issue throughout our careers. Sometimes it functions as designed—the enlightening tool that helps you make a good hire. And sometimes it's the roadblock to diversity.

Says Mitzi:

> In so many instances, "she didn't fit" is another way of saying "she's not like us" and therefore, we are not going to hire or promote her. Oftentimes the "not a good fit" is not accompanied by any commentary related to job competencies or potential. It's like telling your children "because I said so." Diversity of thought comes from diversity of experiences and perspectives, which comes from including and interacting with people who are different from you. Organizations that embrace and proactively include people of diverse backgrounds and perspectives are going to perform far better at addressing the challenges and opportunities of the future than those that don't.

In fact, teams that don't seem to "fit" are often primed to overachieve. Says Angelique:

> I was on a team and our profiles were all over the map— literally an extremely diverse team. This was a team that was known for some significant dysfunction, and we had called in an executive coach to help us. The conclusion was actually

easy for everyone to see—with such a diversity of thought, the tension was going to be obvious in the short term. But everyone agreed—if we can make room for these differences, we would accomplish great things together.

Says Katie:

In most of the places that I've worked, there has been at least the recognition that when hiring we needed to ensure that we were interviewing and considering women and people of color for any open role. But what used to drive me crazy is when we would have an opening in my group, and the hiring managers would interview an appropriate mix of people but then would almost always come in with the recommendation that we hire the guy that looks just like them. And when I would ask about the woman they interviewed, I would get the generic "she wasn't a good fit." I would override when I could, but I learned how critical it was to make sure that the hiring team was diverse. That's not always easy and the more male-dominated the group is, the harder it is to start to change it. In some cases, and we are starting to see this in boards, you just need to mandate that the position be filled by a woman or person of color.

Says Dawn:

She's not a good fit. Or, she's not right for the job. Often this is shorthand for: there is something about her style or personality that is causing them to question her fit for a job. These are real questions that need to be discussed. *But* only after her qualifications for the job have been discussed. Go back to the job specs and ask her experience against the criteria. This may reveal (before a discussion about the softer part of her presence that she is being rejected for) that she actually *is* more qualified. After this acknowledgment, it may be easier to discuss the other elements of her presence and how she conducts herself and question whether being different from the past may be a strength. But getting a conversation to acknowledge the strengths first, always moderates the discussion about the weaknesses.

When I worked at Compton Advertising (now part of Saatchi and Saatchi) on the largest account, P+G, I am told that there was friction around the discussion of whether to put me leading their most important account, Tide laundry detergent. Today I would laugh and reject putting me on a clearly female skewing brand. But at the time, because it was the business most important to P+G, it had only had men in the role. I was the first female account executive to have the job. I am sure there were soft unclear objections to putting me into such an important role. But the leader of the junior development program stated simply: she is the best of her class, and the best should work on the most important account.

When we polled our Gen Z and millennial colleagues, they told us sometimes fit is a concept used to override common sense.

Said one:

> I remember we were hiring for a pretty significant role. And this came up when the hiring committee decided one woman was not a good fit. She was coming from another major brand. She knew her stuff, but they decided she wasn't a good fit. We went around and around about it. Eventually, we did not end up hiring her and we hired this guy who was genuinely not a good fit. I mean, like unequivocally not a good fit. He didn't last a year. The woman went on to another major company. I remember thinking: yeah, she was good enough for them.

How do we deal with the issue of fit?

If it's you . . .

Address the "fit" issues head on. Says Mitzi: Ask the question: What are the characteristics of a "good fitting" candidate? And share how your skills, abilities, and potential match up.

Cie also advises addressing the fit concept during the job hunt:

> Of course, you might sense it, but often it is hard to know if people are questioning your "fit" during the interview process. I had two strategies to try and overcome a potential "fit" issue.
>
> When interviewing if I felt like "other" (whether for being female or gay), I would lean into my strength of being highly collaborative. I would emphasize examples of working extremely well with my own team, with cross-functional

teams and with outside partners. The fact that I worked so well with others made the "not a good fit" argument harder.

I am also aware that people like to hire people they like. Obviously in a work situation you will be spending lots of time with this individual so of course people have a bias with hiring folks they would like to spend time with. So besides demonstrating my professional competence I would put a lot of energy into interesting small talk. I would figure out who was on the interview slate and then gather as much information that would be helpful for small talk. If they went to Notre Dame, I would talk about a big football game coming up. If they used to work in France, I might mention a trip to Paris I recently took. I wanted them to think I would be interesting to talk to on a four-hour flight. To me, overcoming fit was to be both competent and likable.

If you're the boss . . .

When you hear "fit" ask for more information.
Says Lori:

"She's not a good fit" is one of those expressions that is a lazy way of not really describing what is keeping you from moving forward with a particular person. It's similar to other things you'll hear when we cannot put our finger on why, but we just don't want to promote someone. We say things like "she doesn't have executive presence" or "she lacks gravitas" or "I'm not sure about her strategic agility." When I'm in these situations, I say things like, "Let's unpack that; help me understand what you mean by 'good fit.' Let's go back to the hiring criteria we set out. I'd love to go through that with you and look at your notes across the four candidates you interviewed." Similarly, if someone talks about gravitas or executive presence, I ask them to talk about what they mean by executive presence and to give me an example of what it looks like and how it's getting in the way of her performing her job. I try to move from qualitative opinions to demonstrated impact."

Research led by Brian J. Lucas at Cornell University suggests that leaders can neutralize the fit discussion by changing up a common hiring practice: stop asking current employees to come up with an "informal short list" of candidates for a job. When these informal short lists are the first step in the hiring process, the issue of "fit" is baked in from the start. Those lists will likely include individuals who are like the list makers, reflecting their gender and identity. Often lists like these will be drawn up even before a job is formally posted. A leader will likely, intentionally or unintentionally, favor the lists over other candidates. Why? Those individuals will feel like good fits. To guard against fit as a diversity roadblock, leaders must insist the short lists be long lists—drawn not just from those inside the company but outside as well.

When hiring, don't confuse "fit" with "exact match." Says Mitzi: "If you want to assemble a high-performing team, you will want that team to be diverse. So, think of "fit" in terms of who you can add that will provide valuable diverse perspectives and skills. Also, realize that candidates derive leadership skills in different ways, different career paths—you have to ask for and look at transferable skills, not just previous titles and roles."

If you're the witness . . .

When you hear a discussion of fit, good or bad, ask why. Says Lori: "Treat it like any other business comment. Ask questions; ask for specifics; go up to the white board and take notes."

Why is that person a good fit? Why is another person a bad fit? Ask to understand. Probe for data. Use fit as the start of a discussion rather than a reason to end it.

CHAPTER 26

The Good Soldier Trap

How volunteering for low-profile work can hold you back

As we strive to bring change into our workplaces, are we ruining our own career chances in the process? Research suggests the phenomenon of the "good soldier"—the employee who puts time and effort not into personal advancement but advancement for all, may be keeping women back. Why? Working for the betterment of all takes up a whole lot of time.

When we see the problem, we want to fix it, not just for us but for others in the company. We make our case that the changes we want are not simply for our own benefit, but for the advancement of our organization, even our industry. We volunteer, we mentor, we serve on task forces. And that's all good, but research on the good soldier phenomenon shows that we do this while others focus on their own advancement. We may help the company and the industry, but it's at the sacrifice of our own careers.

Research published in *Diverse Issues of Higher Education* shows how this happens. The article looked at Black and Hispanic college faculty and found that they spend twice as much time as their white counterparts mentoring, recruiting, and serving on task forces and committees related to diversity issues. While this certainly benefited the institutions, the faculty members themselves found it took time away from the career-advancing work of publishing.

That put white faculty in a better position to secure tenure. Women face a similar trap. The work they put into improving the environment for women may result in them putting less time into advancing their own careers.

Serve your own needs or serve the company's needs? We've faced the good soldier dilemma many times.

Often it manifests in women asked to take on difficult employees to their team. Says Angelique: "One Good Soldier trap is agreeing to take on the 'problem employees.' Usually, this just creates more work and more headaches and does not result in any extra credit. I once lost months of productivity agreeing to take on a difficult admin."

Says Katie:

> I think when I was most aware of the "Good Soldier" trap was in my role after leaving Pepsi. There seemed to be a lot of cross-functional committees and projects that came up and there was one senior level woman on my team who was almost always volunteered or requested. She was smart, hard-working, reliable, and collegial so she was the perfect team member. I know we teased her about it at the time, but in retrospect I question whether so much "volunteering" was fair to her. When it came time for promotions, I'm not sure she ever got the credit she deserved for how much extra work she did.
>
> Separately, I think Angelique's story about taking on "problem" employees is spot on. The woman I describe above was also a person I could rely on to manage those employees—

either manage them out or turn them around. It was usually managing them out. That is a thankless, difficult task that in a big company takes the willingness and time to document thoroughly and carefully.

Lori describes many of these "good soldier" moments as being "volun-told"—that is, the woman is presented with something that looks like a volunteer opportunity, but she really doesn't have any choice.

And she adds another good soldier example to the mix: women are often asked to handle difficult conversations.

> I once had to talk to one woman about her short skirts and another woman about her alleged affair with another senior executive. In the first case, I was asked to give some nuanced coaching to a colleague, and the reason was that it would be creepy coming from her male boss.
>
> In the second case, an executive came over to work for me, and everyone talked openly that she was allegedly having an affair with an SVP. I was told that it was hurting her reputation and that I had to tell her that everyone was talking about her situation. The part that annoyed me was that she'd worked for a very senior man for the prior two years, and once again, he didn't say anything because "it would be creepy coming from a male boss."
>
> The question this raises—do we let women not just do the housework in the office but also have all the discussions that are difficult?

Mitzi says yes. She recalls a woman in her professional circle who successfully navigated several tough conversations—and then became everyone's favorite coach on the topic of tough conversations. The issue became her special burden. "She was so good at it that she became the 'go to' person to have or to prep others for having the difficult conversations."

Our younger colleagues are also noting these same pitfalls.

> I've noticed a couple of phenomena. One is that there seems to be some tacit agreement that women are the go-to's for any task that's about relationships, communication, or managing people. Not only does this sell men short—it's not like they aren't able to communicate—but it's incredibly time consuming. Every time I'm asked to go smooth out some conflict between two co-workers I'm taking time away from other work I'd rather focus on, work that affects the bottom line. Secondly, I noticed that men, for the most part, seem to be better at saying no. If a guy is asked to go smooth out that same conflict, they seem to feel fine just saying no and redirecting back to a woman who'll be "better at it anyway." They don't feel guilty about it because they seem to feel sure that it's isn't their job.

There is additional pressure on women when the good soldier projects are ones they believe in.

Says Mitzi:

> Many do work for the good of the company or company culture beyond your day job by participating in "affinity groups." If you've been in one or a part of one, you

know they are extremely valuable to the constituents in terms of being a network of support and mentorship. Often the support, coaching, development, and mentorship received in the affinity groups goes a long way to help a company retain its key talent and affinity group members are often involved in helping the companies recruit talent. In addition, companies benefit from the role affinity groups play organizing cultural days/events to educate and celebrate different cultures (Black History Month, Cinco de Mayo, etc.) and from the unofficial advisory role members play on an assortment of business topics—including product development and promotions, civic events. Rarely does this extra time and effort show up on your performance review—you do it because you're a part of the community and it's the right thing to do. It is part of the work that makes the company better.

I coached a female leader who shared how she was heavily engaged in an affinity group. It was important to her because she benefited from the network of support and ideas as she navigated her professional and personal situation. That said, in talking with one of her mentors, he talked about how she should focus on the things that were more closely aligned to her client.

It's not always an easy knot to unravel.
How to handle . . .

If it's you . . .

Don't automatically say yes. Too often, women agree rather than push back. This can have long-term consequences. Says Angelique:

> This goes wrong when you agree to a deliverable even when you have not been given the proper resources—people, money, and/or time. You are asked to "figure it out," so as a good soldier, you and your team work longer hours to make up for the lack of time or additional people. You get the deliverable completed, but that just makes it harder to believe you need the resources next time. I recall being told by my work friends (and my husband) you just have to tell them no, you can't do it. If you don't get it done, they will believe that you needed the resources. If only that wasn't so hard in practice.

It's also important to note that not all good soldier work is damaging. There are times when it works to your benefit. Says Cie:

> My management style fostered a very open-door policy. It was hugely beneficial and encouraged people to feel very comfortable bopping into my office and sharing ideas or giving me a heads-up on potential issues. That same open-door policy also resulted in many people coming to ask career advice, so I spent a significant amount of time being a sounding board for a variety of issues. Ninety-five percent of the time, these conversations were not in any official mentoring capacity so there was no credit as one of my deliverables of my job. But I was happy to do it and think it was an important aspect of being a leader and giving back. Many of those relationships

have continued to this day and some of those individuals I consider lifelong friends.

If you're the boss . . .

Monitor to see that women are not doing all the good soldier work. Be aware of your own actions and ensure you're not only nominating women for various task force assignments, etc. The jobs of culture and talent development belong to all leaders. The role of volunteer for an office event is one that should rotate through the ranks. If you tap someone for a volunteer job, consider how it will be interpreted.

Make note of the good soldier work when it's time for salary reviews. Recognize work that is benefiting the company as a whole.

Cie says far too often, managers know perfectly well they're leveraging the good soldier mindset, but they don't feel pressure to change.

> At my first job out of graduate school one of my early bosses told me a goat analogy that really stuck with me. When trying to get to the top of the hill, it is a safer bet to add one more saddle to a good goat, one that is already carrying a big load, than to add that saddle to an average goat even if it is carrying less. That is because the good goat always pulls through and the average goat may or may not. An employee known as a "good goat" will always get a disproportionate amount of the workload. When a boss has to delegate assignments they will tend to add more to a "good goat" employee even if they are overburdened, rather than an employee that has capacity but is not considered as reliable. Bosses should consider this when handing out work across their teams. Make

sure you do not always burden the very high-performing employees with more of the non-critical office housework.

If you're the witness . . .

If you see this—but you're not usually asked to handle the good soldier efforts—then it's long past time you volunteered. The opportunities may be visible—an annual United Way campaign or an announced committee. Others may be off the radar. Let your boss know you're available to pitch in.

CHAPTER 27

Not Just Mentors—Get Sponsors

The trick for successfully moving up the corporate ladder

Many of us over the years have had mentors—individuals who advised us, coached us, answered our questions. These are people with whom we forged close personal bonds. They have been our shoulders to cry on, our sounding boards, our guides.

And they were not enough.

Firms and industries struggling to understand why their progress promoting women has not been better have uncovered a fault in the mentorship model. While a mentor can be a positive, nurturing relationship, often a mentor cannot get you promoted.

For that you need a sponsor.

There is a big difference between a mentor and a sponsor. The difference is so significant, it's a reason women are filling the ranks of corporate America and yet still failing to move into senior leadership roles. Mentor and sponsor are not the same, points out "Sponsoring Women to Success" a report by Catalyst. And the difference between the two can be summed up in one word: power.

"While a mentor may be a sponsor, sponsors go beyond the traditional social, emotional and personal growth development provided by many mentors," write report co-authors Heather Foust-Cummings,

Sarah Dinolfo and Jennifer Kohler. "Sponsorship is focused on advancement and predicated on power."

While we may have mentors, when we lack sponsors, we lack access to the power structure.

A sponsor can put a name forward for a promotion, lobby to get someone into a leadership role, and at the highest levels, hire and promote. While both men and women have mentors, men are more likely than women to have sponsors. Without sponsors, women are shut out of the leadership pipeline.

Angelique saw this firsthand, when she returned from maternity leave and found she had to rebuild the momentum she'd had in her pre-motherhood days. "I thought I could just do good work and have the opportunities and promotions come. It took years for me to realize that those who were advancing were not only doing good work, but they were actively *selling* their work. They were seeking forums to showcase what they were doing. They were seeking out sponsors," she says.

It was her wake-up call to find a sponsor herself. "I can recall managers who would tell me my work was fantastic, but when it came to plum assignments, or promotion, or elite committees, or executive coaching, I wasn't getting enough of them. I realized I was missing a trick."

Katie saw the impact sponsors had on her career.

> I credit virtually all of my career success to being fortunate enough to have had great sponsors. Some were (and are) women, and some were men. Early in my career, when I hoped to transfer between divisions at PepsiCo, my boss (a woman) at the time pulled the "behind the scenes" informal strings to help make it happen. While at Pepsi, Dawn Hudson and Dave Burwick gave me huge opportunities and challenging roles.

After I left Pepsi, I went to ESPN where I worked for a guy who supported me 110 percent. He made sure I was in the right meetings, put me on industry committees to increase my profile, and got me a very prestigious role in the company's annual planning process. He also signed me up for a very selective program run by Disney, which owned ESPN, that sent me on a ten-day immersive experience with 25 other top-level Disney employees to gain in-depth experience across the company. I was one of three ESPN employees sent and I had worked there for all of three months. It was his sponsorship that made that happen.

A rising leader we interviewed said that sponsorship was talked about in their companies but was still difficult for women to achieve:

> I absolutely believe that there is a lot of pressure for companies to identify and cultivate diverse talent. Some of it may be bowing to societal pressures but I think a lot of it is sincere. The problem is that the most effective sponsorships still seem to be the ones that develop organically and comfortably, i.e., when an up-ladder man sees a younger down-ladder man who reminds him of a younger version of himself and he plucks him out of the crowd. It's harder when these relationships have to be reimagined.

Why are women not securing sponsors at the same rate as men? A study by researchers at Rutgers University and Johns Hopkins looked at the role of sponsorship in academic medicine. The research team suggests that women may not be as aware of the importance of power networks and therefore choose mentors who are not able to serve as sponsors. What's more, they say, women are more likely to prefer other women as mentors. That can mean they are connected to fewer high-level leadership relationships with the power and influence to act as sponsors.

Another point from the research team that backs up Angelique's experience: women, the researchers say, may be uncomfortable with self-promotion, preferring their work to speak for itself. They may also be concerned about what they called the "double bind" women face in which they experience backlash for appearing too ambitious. Whatever the motivation may be, when women hold back, they are less likely to be spotted by a sponsor as a high potential candidate. To get a good sponsor, they wrote, a protégée must be "seen."

Another, more recent wrinkle in the sponsorship saga comes from the ripple effect of the #MeToo movement. An article published in *Global Law and Business* suggests that women in law are having more trouble attracting sponsors because men are fearful of the frequent and closer personal interactions a sponsorship bond would demand. A January 2018 poll found nearly 30 percent of male managers are uncomfortable working alone with a woman. The number of men uncomfortable mentoring a woman tripled from 5 to 16 percent. In a separate online survey, senior men said they were more hesitant than they used to be about having a work dinner with a junior woman. They expressed even more concern about traveling for work with a junior woman. Substantial numbers of men say they are more nervous about entering into a closer professional relationship with women. And both men and women in the surveys acknowledge that these sorts of professional relationships are at risk because of the perception that unacceptable behavior could be occurring.

In our experience, sponsors are not in the same category as mentors—and this is a nuance that many often miss. You may be assigned a mentor. You can hire a coach. But a sponsor is a different kind of relationship. It's one that you can't simply reach for. It must be earned. A sponsor is someone who will vouch for you, put their own reputation on the line for you. That requires a relationship of trust. Your sponsor must be certain that you will deliver.

That can put women and people of color at a disadvantage. A man may be able to leverage a personal relationship—perhaps through a sports team or other extracurricular activity—and seek to build that into a sponsorship relationship. A woman who does not have the outside office friendship option may need to take a different route to securing a sponsor—she will need to find other ways to build a relationship of mutual trust. But it is a goal worth pursuing. A sponsor can be the reason your name comes up at the talent meeting as someone ready for a promotion. A lack of sponsorship may be the reason you are someone the leadership respects but doesn't know well enough to promote. Sponsors can move your career.

How to manage the issue of mentors and sponsors.

If it's you . . .

Know what you are currently getting . . . and what you still need. The people who help us along the way often do not wear name tags indicating their roles in our lives. We need to understand what they are able to provide for us and at the same time, understand the gaps we may need to proactively fill. Try sorting supporters into three buckets: coaches, mentors, and sponsors. A coach is someone who helps with a specific task. So, you may have a coach who helps you acquire a new skill or advance in an area in which you have some basic training. A coach is a paid role and your relationship with the coach may run only as long as the learning process takes.

A mentor can be at any level of the corporate hierarchy. The job is usually unpaid and it's designed to give you a role model, emotional support, and feedback on how to improve.

Finally, a sponsor has several key elements that differentiate from the coach and mentor. A sponsor must be a senior manager with influence. A sponsor is someone who fights to get their protégée promoted and who makes sure the protégée is considered for promising opportunities and challenging assignments.

Coaches help you. Mentors give you support and encouragement. Sponsors invest in you. Ask yourself: Are you getting all three? What are you missing?

Cie offers this piece of advice on how to connect with a potential sponsor: "If you see someone who is naturally good at sponsoring talent, try to work on their team and get to know them. Sponsorship is not a zero-sum game for great leaders. When someone is good at it with one person, chances are they are good at it in general."

And Lori makes room for the fact that you may not always *like* your sponsor:

> A sponsor doesn't always look like it does on TV. Two of my biggest sponsors in my career were people that were really tough on me. They pushed and pushed me, and it was only years later that I realized that they saw more potential in me than I even saw in myself. The learning here is don't mistake kindness for sponsorship. I've worked for many nice people who never lifted a finger to help me break through.

Mitzi says:

Recognize that the rate of your career advancement is highly correlated with the amount of sponsorship you receive. Many have heard the phrase "It's not what you know but who you know." In reality, there's more. It's not just about who you know, but who knows you and who is willing to put their reputation on the line for you. Ask yourself if the people making and influencing the decisions about who gets the job you want would say yes—you're the right person for that job. Would they advocate publicly on your behalf? I also think it's important to think proactively about where you might have sponsorship gaps and create a plan to close the gaps—ahead of the need.

If you're the boss . . .

When you're in charge, ensure that expectations around mentorship and sponsorship are explicit. There should be no confusion as to whether or not women should be sponsored at the same rate as men. Consider including sponsorship duties in the annual reviews of senior managers so that the practice is measured and rewarded. Systemize the sponsorship process and use technology to understand who on the team has a sponsor (and who does not) and further engage technology to track the goals and achievements of protégées.

Also, suggests Ida Abbott, author of the *Global Law and Business* article, look for new models that might expand and improve female employees' access to sponsorship. One company developed a nine-month leadership development course for women in which each participant was assigned a sponsor. Another firm created what it called a "triad mentoring program," open to all associates, that groups lawyers into triads of mentee, mentor, and sponsor from a senior leadership role. Still another is experimenting with a team approach to sponsorship, in which each protégée is assigned a primary sponsor and additional sponsors from other parts of the firm as part of that individual's team.

Mitzi thinks of this from a perspective of legacy—what do you want to be known for?

> Every year, during the Super Bowl week or game each head coach is usually featured. In particular, I remember the stories about Bill Belichick, Andy Reid, and Tony Dungy— and the impact they have had on the ranks of coaching. Quite often a visual of a "family tree" would be shown that lists all of the head coaches, offensive and defensive coordinators, and assistant coaches that were on their respective staffs. So, the question for bosses and leaders is: What does your sponsorship tree look like? Are there women on your tree? Are there women of color on your tree? When people think about you as a leader, do they talk about the impact you have had on a business's most precious assets—the human capital?

Finally, reach out to coach others on the difference between mentors and sponsors. Says Angelique:

> One time a young woman told me about a mentorship program where she was assigned to a senior male mentor, as part of an effort to help rising leaders connect with established leaders.

She told me it didn't feel like a mentorship, as she didn't feel connected to this man—he didn't seem that interested in who she actually was, but was more interested in giving her advice in general. As a mentorship, it felt forced. I told her about the difference between mentorship and sponsorship, and I said, "What if you used this opportunity to make sure he knows what you are working on, and can speak in support of your work in other forums?" This seemed to be a light bulb for her, as she could see the difference and the value in that visibility of her work with someone already in power.

If you're the witness . . .

If you're in a senior position, offer to be a sponsor to a woman or minority in your company. Be willing not just to act as a sounding board or role model, but be willing to invest in the individual and commit to helping that person advance.

If you're a witness in a senior leadership position, consider whether or not you and your organization are sponsoring women consistent with how you are sponsoring men. Do the numbers reflect your efforts? If the answer is yes, who can you share your success and best practices with? If the answer is no, what can you commit to in order to change the situation?

If you're not at a senior level (yet!), advocate for organized sponsorship effort at your company and give voice to the concerns that it's a critical advancement tool available primarily to white men. Open the discussion on ways to make sponsorship available to all.

Section Six

Personal Space

In a diverse workplace, there are bound to be times when awkward situations occur. These are the interactions that may seem small or insignificant, but gather to create a feeling of other-ness that we want to dispel.

CHAPTER 28

Awkward Chivalry

What to do when good manners turn into cringe moments

Lori was at a recent board meeting; she was one of two women at a table dominated by men. As the board did business, at one point the conversation turned to a man who was not present at the meeting, but whose actions could have consequences for the company. Several board members expressed concern about this individual. And then one man at the table said this: "You know, the truth of the matter is that this guy—excuse me, ladies—really needs to grow a pair!"

Lori knew she was supposed to smile demurely at his apologetic aside. But she was busy fighting back the urge to say: "Why exactly did you feel the need to apologize to me just now? Were you worried that you upset me by referencing testicles?"

But she didn't. She just filed it away as one of the many instances of gender bias that no one seems to mention. This one in particular is one we call "awkward chivalry." That's the phrase we use for behavior that men somehow think is polite, but in fact, simply reinforces women as "others" in a corporate setting.

Often this kind of behavior is cloaked in an air of manners. It's behavior that many may consider gentlemanly. Awkward chivalry often creeps into the language of the workplace and into conversations men may consider complimentary. But in fact, when this sort of throwback behavior takes place, it sets women apart from the group and makes it that much harder for them to be considered equal to their male colleagues.

Truth be told, we struggled ourselves to define awkward chivalry in a concrete way. We debated the examples over and over and found that one woman's awkward chivalry is another woman's shrug. Lori and Angelique find it irritating when ten guys squish against the walls of an elevator so that a woman can exit first. Cie doesn't find that clearcut annoying. "Depends on the circumstances," she says. Some of us cringe when men stand up when a woman enters the room. Katie, who was raised in Virginia, says that's just Southern manners. Most of us hate the fact that a man will shake hands with all the men in a room, but when he comes to a woman, he'll go for a hug or a peck on the cheek. Dawn's willing to give that a pass. All of us are just fine with men helping us get our bags into a plane's overhead compartment. But we're split on the habit of men sprinting ahead to open a door or diving for a business dinner check.

With such variance in opinions, why bother to write about the topic at all?

The reason, we decided, is because no matter what your own personal definition of awkward chivalry may be, its existence in the workplace is a factor in women's advancement. These acts of old-time *politesse* may be decent in intention but problematic in effect. They serve to highlight the fact that men see women differently.

Professors Peter Glick of Lawrence University and Susan T. Fiske of Princeton pioneered the discussion of this problem and back in the early 90s, gave it a name: "ambivalent sexism." The practitioners were not uniformly against women. In many cases, they admired and respected the women involved. But they also held sexist ideas about the role of women in their minds and this seeped into their actions with women in the workplace. This mix of emotions spills out in two primary ways, the researchers found. There's "hostile sexism," in which a man might openly say women are not as smart as men and therefore should not be promoted. Then there's "benevolent sexism," in which the behavior seems to stem from good intentions, but ends up nega-tively impacting women anyway. For example, responding to a female colleague's strong negotiating skills with the phrase, "You're tough, for a girl!" Sort of a compliment. But really not.

We may be inclined to give men a pass when they engage in benev-olent sexism, since it may seem like a well-intentioned accident. But Glick and Fiske don't. Hostile sexism and benevolent sexism are two sides of the same sexist coin, they say. Benevolent sexism is the way men try to entice women into remaining in traditional roles—an effort to get women to "stay in their lane" and not fully integrate into the male workplace. Hostile sexism is what often follows when a woman does not respond to the cues in the benevolent sexism. But both are tactics men use to maintain a gender status quo in which they lead and women follow.

Benevolent sexism presents a problem for women in the work-place, not just because it can lead to more hostile behavior, but because it has its own negative impact. A study published in the *Journal of*

Personality and Social Psychology found benevolent sexism negatively affected women's performance. When exposed to this behavior, women increasingly doubted their own abilities and self-worth. Benevolent sexism sounds inoffensive, even positive, when it's delivered, but in fact, it's insidious and damaging to women, the study found.

We've seen this phenomenon.

Says Cie:

> I find it irritating and condescending when men swear and then turn to a woman or women and say "pardon my French." I dislike this for several reasons. It calls attention to the women as "not equal"—like some delicate flower that needs to be shielded and protected. Or it makes us seem like an "other." It also smacks of *"us men would be having more fun and more real and interesting conversation if you were not here,"* and pushes women further out of the conversation.
>
> Many women swear too—so we do not need to be called out as a special protected class.

And Angelique:

> I have struggled with the small gestures of chivalry in the workplace, because I know the intention is good, but it feels way more harmful than men realize. As a new executive on a leadership team reporting to the CEO, I was thrilled to be seen as an equal among the C-suite. It was a friendly group of nine, with three women and several men of color. However, it was frequent that a subgroup would meet and I would be the only woman in the room.

The regular banter would be friendly and casual, and inevitably a man would swear and then turn to me and apologize—"pardon my French." I know the intention was to be polite and chivalrous, but it made me feel like I didn't belong in that room. It was never about seniority, as we were all equals on that front—it was only about gender, and that felt awful. The implication is I shouldn't be hearing that conversation unfiltered—really, I shouldn't be in that room, I couldn't handle the "real talk."

It's especially noticeable when men think—or at least appear to think—that they're giving a compliment. So, when Lori was recently added to a new board, a man congratulated her and then added: "It's such a great time for women to land board roles." He may have thought that sounded like a positive statement. To Lori, it landed like a qualifier. "It suggested that maybe I wouldn't have gotten that spot were I not a woman," she says. "It sounded positive on its face, but the underlying suggestion is that I, alone, without my gender advantage, would not have been enough."

Indeed, our Gen Z and millennial colleagues said they noticed awkward chivalry most often when it was couched in a compliment.

I was on a Zoom call with one of my distributors and the man was introducing me to my new brand manager/primary contact. At one point, he said "Don't be fooled by that smile, she is a shark! That's why she got to where she is today." I was taken off guard and very taken aback, because everyone on the call seemed pretty culturally sensitive to women's equality and women's rights. It wasn't the old school sales people or the super misogynistic guys that I've dealt with in the past and would expect this from. That type of behavior has been used *so many* times with me in the sales world. When I started sales, they called me "the pit bull." As I've increasingly risen in rank in companies I've worked for, my male bosses have had to introduce me to my new contacts at distributors or suppliers and I often get "Don't be fooled by her appearance/smile/sweetness, she is a killer, or a pit bull, or a hunter." It's basically alluding to the fact that I look cute and innocent—or dumb/not able to do my job to a high standard—but, surprise!, I am actually good at what I do. The people who say it are the people who think they are applauding women in power and women's equality. It's the people who think they are allies, when in fact they are participating in one of the most slap-in-the-face microaggressions that I have ever experienced.

To be sure, not all polite behavior is unwelcome. One of our younger colleagues says she notices when men hold a door for her. "I think it's nice." But it's an irritant we encounter regularly. Says Angelique: "My business school friends and I were out to dinner and they were insisting on paying the check, and I know they were struggling with the attempt to be chivalrous (I was the only woman), but I had to literally point out that we were not on a date, and I wanted to be treated as an equal."

How to handle awkward chivalry . . .

If it's you . . .

Cie has a go-to response when a man curses and apologizes. "I say: 'No fucking problem.' That usually does the trick."

When you can spot the awkward action ramping up, it makes sense to be proactive, says Lori. In the case of the handshake versus hug, see if you can get out ahead of the awkward moment. "I might say: 'My post-COVID self is neither hugging nor shaking.' And then I'd do the elbow bump with a huge smile."

But sometimes a more direct—and less humorous—approach is called for. Cie recalls a colleague who joined a new company in a senior position. When introducing her to the team, her new male colleague said: "This is our new boss. I've known her for a long time and I assure you she's the right man for the job!" The line got a laugh and Cie's colleague smiled through it. But afterwards she took the man aside and said: "Never. Ever. Introduce me like that again."

It may take time and effort for the men to understand that what they are saying is not complimentary and, in fact, "others" the women in a way that undermines them.

If you're the boss . . .

Model appropriate language. Correct stereotypical behavior, even if it seems benevolent in its delivery.

Angelique had this experience in a review process.

In 360-degree feedback, a senior man was trying to give a compliment to a junior woman who works with him on a cross-functional project. He wrote: "As a young woman with important responsibilities, she has shown that a female can and does perform 100 percent as effectively as any other top performing employee . . ."

Good intention—but expressing surprise that a woman is just as good as "any other top performing employee" is not exactly a compliment.

Consider a meeting with your team (or division or company) to discuss the issue openly. Let men ask questions "should I open the door for you?" and let women state preferences or their own questions: "I would appreciate it if we make greetings gender neutral—e.g., if you shake men's hands, shake mine; if you fist bump, do the same with me."

If you're the witness . . .

Call out the "othering" when you hear it. To the man above who penned the benevolently sexist 360-degree review, you might say: Why does that surprise you? How did you expect her to perform? Why do you feel the need to hold her apart as "a female" rather than a colleague?

Ask a woman how she feels about it. Bring the topic into open discussion.

Ensure that your own behavior is gender neutral—if you hold open a door, you do it for both women and men.

Use real language, not platitudes or clichés, to describe co-workers. You don't need to say: "Though she be but little, she is fierce." You can just say: "She is fierce." Stick to the facts of your statement and don't try to dress it up—even with a little Shakespeare.

CHAPTER 29

Absent Eye Contact

How to handle when you can't get the guys to meet your eyes

There are professional moments when we know it's all working for us. Perhaps we are presenting to an audience, addressing a meeting or even just walking the halls. We know it's all working because we can see it in their eyes. Their eyes are on us.

Conversely, when their eyes drop to their iPhones during our presentations, when they're shuffling papers while we're speaking, or when they avoid our eyes when we pass in the hall, we suspect the message is negative: we're not important.

Eye contact is a critical aspect of non-verbal communication. In our daily lives, we encounter it all the time and it's often not hard to decipher. We know what a wink means. What an eye roll means. What a glare means. In all these cases, the eyes are easy to read.

But in the office, eye contact becomes more complex. What does it mean when he won't meet my eyes when we pass in the hall? How do I interpret the fact that he often looks away while I'm speaking?

It's complicated.

But it's not going unnoticed. Lack of eye contact is often cited by women when they feel they are not being taken seriously by their male co-workers, says Audrey Nelson, Phd, in her article "The Politics of Eye Contact: A Gender Perspective," published in *Psychology Today*. When a man fails to make eye contact, women perceive this as a signal that he does not respect her as an equal.

Is this true?

Maybe.

The *Journal of Image and Vision Computing* released research that suggests that people pay more attention—and give more eye contact—to a conversation partner they consider to be of higher status. In another study published by the *Journal of Nonverbal Behavior,* those considered influential will get more eye contact in a meeting than those considered less influential.

Still, science is hardly settled on the topic. Researchers agree that both men and women can and do engage in what's known as visual dominance. But they also acknowledge that non-verbal behaviors are tricky and often cannot be mapped with scientific certainty. A look away may have meaning. Or it may not.

But science aside, we're aware that eye contact is part of the communication process of the workplace. Use of eye contact as a power play may not be well mapped by the scientific community. But we know it when we see it.

Angelique's POV:

Just for the academic interest of it, I started to pay attention to how often the men would look me in the eye versus my female counterparts. It always seemed way less than even, but maybe it was just me.

I was in a meeting once where I was the most senior person in the room, and I had a male and female colleague with me, and we were speaking with our agency representatives—one male and one female. It was bugging me that my male colleague was only looking at the other man when he spoke, but I thought maybe I'm being paranoid, maybe it was just me.

Then we took a bathroom break and the two men left the room and the other women immediately said to me "Gee, it's as if we aren't in the room!" I realized it isn't just me!

Cie also wondered if she was the only one who noticed.

I wondered if maybe I was paranoid about the eye contact issue and similar to Angelique. I discovered many women who were also sensitive to it and all found it very disempowering. At times I would be so preoccupied by it—I would be so focused on the lack of eye contact—that it actually prevented me being fully engaged in the meeting. Of course, not being engaged in the meeting would lead to contributing less, which of course would naturally lead to receiving less eye contact—very bad cycle.

Our millennial and Gen Z colleagues picked up on it, too.

> I noticed it, 100 percent. Not from my team members spe-
> cifically, but others. My first six months at this firm, I didn't get
> eye contact from a lot of men. I didn't know what to do. Was it
> because I was a woman? Was it because I was a Black woman?
> I had all these thoughts in my head. I would walk in the hall-
> ways, and they would turn their heads so they wouldn't have
> to make eye contact with me. It was something that weighed
> on me. I thought: What kind of place is this?

The controversy around #MeToo and other forms of sexual harassment also plays a role. Surveys have even shown men are worried
about being alone with a female colleague for fear of being accused of
harassment. Men may avoid eye contact to avoid any misconception
of romantic interest. But that's a relatively recent flashpoint and most of
us have noticed the lack of eye contact issue well before sexual harassment was in the news.

And some suggest this is a manifestation in the different ways men
and women communicate. Katie says:

> I once attended a conference focused on inclusion. I
> remember one of the speakers discussing how men and wom-
> en's communication styles can cause misunderstandings in
> the workplace. They described two men having a conversation
> where they stand shoulder to shoulder just slightly angled
> towards each other—they speak *to* each other but they don't
> look directly *at* each other the whole time. Women, however,
> face each other directly and look each other in the eye. Where

it gets almost comical is when they role-played a woman trying to have a direct conversation with a man and he kept turning a few degrees to have the type of conversation he wants to have while she basically follows him around in a circle.

And Mitzi wonders if the lack of eye contact she's experienced has been less about gender and more about power.

I experienced the lack of eye contact most frequently early in my career when I was in sales roles. At the time, I thought of the eye slight more in the "power" context—hierarchical position. I would be in the room with customers/clients and our respective leaders, and all eyes would be on the more senior leaders. The eyes follow the money and the person with the highest approving power—the most senior person.

How can you handle the eye contact issue?

If it's you . . .

Use your words. After noticing the behavior and hearing confirmation from the other women in the agency meeting, Angelique opted to name the problem: "When we resumed the meeting and the behavior continued, I found a way to say 'Well, I assume you would really look to me when you ask that question because I would be accountable for that next step,' and I emphasized the word *look*. My colleague apologized and said, 'Oh, I didn't mean to be looking anywhere in particular.'"

Mitzi also uses voice. "I've also found that the eyes follow the speaker. So, it has been important for me to speak up and to share my point of view in general, and especially, if I was the only woman or person of color in the room."

Cie has developed some meeting strategies to address this point. "Where you sit in a meeting can help. I would try and get to meetings early so I could position myself near the key players and not get stuck down at the end of the table. Also, contribute early and often—assuming, of course, you have valuable things to say and are not just talking to talk. That way you are immediately part of the key discussion."

Dawn suggests acknowledging the awkwardness men may feel, making eye contact with a woman in the age of #MeToo. The men need to know the ground rules, she says. "To the men in the room, you may feel awkward in today's environment looking directly at a woman lest you be seen to be 'eyeing' her. Know that eye contact is welcome and a form of respect, not disrespect. And feel free to laugh with the women and share jokes too. They just want an equal seat at the table. But we do realize in this #MeToo world it can be intimidating for men."

If you're the boss . . .

Keep in mind that your eye contact matters. The team will notice where your eyes travel during meetings. Individuals will notice when you look at them—and when you don't. Your eye-contact behavior will be noticed, discussed and gossiped over by everyone looking for signs of who is in favor and who is not. Be a role model and make an effort to look at everyone to make everyone feel respected, heard, and brought into the conversation. Be aware and ensure that your eyes are traveling with intention.

Also, some cultures interpret eye contact in different ways. If you suspect a cultural misunderstanding, acknowledge it and ensure all parties are aware of the different interpretations.

If you're the witness . . .

Be aware of your own eye-contact trends and consider whether or not you are looking with equality. If you are one of the senior people in the room, know that eye contact goes a long way to making people feel included. Try to look around when you speak.

CHAPTER 30

Awkwork: Is This a Meeting or a Date?

How to handle the blurring of social and professional conversations

t's no secret that work life and personal life often overlap. But we can see that separation getting blurrier every day.

Consider the following scenarios:

- A team member approaches you during the work day and suggests you meet after work to "get drinks."
- You're at a networking event and you connect with a smart, attractive client who asks for your contact info. The next day, you get a text suggesting a meetup at a bar.
- You used social media to advance your professional networking footprint. Now someone you've met on LinkedIn wants to meet in real life.

Are these meetings? Or are these dates?

In the era of social media, 24/7 work and routine job-changing, that can be a very hard question to answer.

Making connections is a primary way anyone moves ahead in today's business world. We are encouraged to network and engage and create a matrix of individuals we can tap for support, advice, even a job or promotion. Using social capital for career advancement is an effective tool.

What's more, many of us will find our friends, even our spouses, via work engagements. It's hardly unusual for someone to look across a sea of cubicles and find love. We spend so much time at our jobs, it stands to reason that we would connect with our colleagues as people. Not always, not all colleagues, but it happens.

That being said, how can women handle the meeting/date confusion? How can we navigate the tricky, sometimes sticky situations to our advantage and ensure that no one ends ups in HR making or defending against a #MeToo complaint?

The impact of the #MeToo controversy has some men saying they're avoiding women in the workplace. A study out of the University of Nevada at Las Vegas found 20 percent of men in a survey were uncomfortable working alone with a woman in a private office or conference room, 40 percent said they were uncomfortable socializing with female colleagues outside of work and 26 percent said they were uncomfortable traveling with a woman for work. Male concern about harassment claims extends to a reluctance to hire and mentor women.

And then there is the very real concern about sexual assault. If a woman accepts an invitation for drinks or is alone with a male colleague in his hotel room, has she sent a signal that she considers it a date? For all the stories about harmless flirtation, there are plenty that feature men like film producer and convicted sex offender Harvey Weinstein, who used his professional sphere to lure and assault women.

Avoiding the opposite sex at work is not an answer. We need a more holistic approach. We've seen the problems that this lack of clarity can cause.

Says Cie:

> One of my peers was asked by a fellow director in the marketing department to go out to dinner. For a week she talked about this, trying to figure out if it was a date (which she was not interested in) or just two colleagues grabbing dinner (which she was interested in).
>
> The dinner ended up being two coworkers talking over dinner. But she spent a week ruminating over his intentions and worried about potentially sending the wrong signal.
>
> An invitation by a coworker for drinks or dinner can easily be wrongly perceived as a date. This situation used to raise more red flags with women, invited by male coworkers, but now, in the #MeToo era, some men now find it equally awkward to extend an invitation to a woman fearing that it may be misinterpreted. So, this dynamic is lose-lose. Women miss out on informal networking, which can be pivotal to building strong relationships as well as be instrumental to getting on equal footing with male coworkers. Men miss out on getting to know half the workforce better and therefore are less comfortable in recommending women whom they do not know as well.

Says Angelique:

> I feel so torn about being invited to go drinking with the guys. It takes extra thought to ensure the invitation feels safe, and usually that leads to not being invited at all.

On one business trip I stopped by my boss's room to pick him up for an evening event, as we had agreed. When I got there, he suggested we not be early, and invited me to open a bottle of wine with him in his suite. On the one hand, I was happy to be able to get this bonding time with my boss! If I were a guy, it's the perfect chance to share ideas and build our relationship. On the other hand—was it weird? I was probably a little too conscious of where I sat, how much I drank, how long we stayed there. It turned out fine, perfectly professional, nothing at all happened that wouldn't happen if we were in public. But it was definitely not an easy moment to feel the normal bonding with the boss that I'm sure a man would have felt.

In hindsight, I wish I had been able to pretend we were two male colleagues (or two female colleagues) having a very expected conversation. It would have probably enabled me to feel much more relaxed and enjoy the opportunity to bend my boss's ear. Or perhaps I might have been bolder to help my boss see how to make that a safer moment. Maybe something more direct like, "Well, boss, we'll just pretend I'm a guy and this is not at all weird."

What can we do to make it all less weird?

If it's you . . .

Lori says:

As I evaluate situations like the one Angelique described, I take myself out of the story and think about what I would want my 24-year-old daughter to do in this situation. Ninety-nine point nine nine nine percent of colleagues in America will *not* turn out to be Harvey Weinstein or Jeffrey Epstein, but the sad truth is that the ones who do turn out to be those villains usually don't hold up signs alerting you to the danger. So, here's a suggestion, if the boss asks you to come for a glass of wine, say, "I would love a glass of wine; can we go down to the hotel bar and grab one there? You know these crazy colleagues of ours; if they see me coming out of your room, they'll be distracted and gossiping for weeks to come." Remember: it's not just keeping yourself safe from potential awkward moments; it's also keeping your reputation safe.

When possible, try to keep your sense of humor. Says Katie:

I was single at the time but at a fairly senior level at Pepsi (VP). There was a regional sales guy, junior to me, who lived in another city and was coming up to headquarters. He had mentioned at one point that he had a brother or someone he wanted to fix me up with. He came to town and claimed to be setting up a get-together and invited me and, I thought, several of my colleagues. I showed up and found that it was just me. He didn't scare me because it was a public place and he had no power over my career but I also didn't feel like I could just walk out without looking like a jerk. So, I sat down for a drink and then was going to leave. He proceeded to try and get me to drink tequila shots (I declined) and pitched me on the idea of having him as an "out of town" boyfriend (he was married). I declined that offer, too. I found the whole thing fairly laughable and I remember telling Cie about it the next day—just the balls of a guy trying to proposition an employee senior to him in such a ridiculous way.

One of our younger colleagues used this strategy: if someone asked her to dinner and she wasn't sure if it was a request for a date, she would just say, "Yes, that sounds fun; I'll grab Jane, too, and we'll have a fun night out." By inviting another coworker, she diffused the situation, but also allowed herself to get to know the person who asked her.

And another we interviewed said she wore a fake engagement ring a lot to dissuade the weird ambiguous dinner/drink requests.

If you're the boss . . .

Be clear about the rules around socializing outside of work. Talk about the issue to bring it out into the open and avoid misunderstanding.

Also, be creative and test out new tools to see if there are ways to make connections without misunderstanding. Says Angelique:

Post-COVID, one element that seems to be reset is the forums for socializing and networking. As these forums move online, they also become safer and easier to keep professional. One virtual networking event I enjoyed was a Zoom meeting put together with a set of former colleagues of mine from Pepsi. We all worked together on the SoBe brand team, and it really was a dream team at the time. These colleagues are almost all at other companies now, and the breadth of perspective is tremendous—including senior positions in Target, Marriott, Nike, NFL, myself at BlackRock and a few still at Pepsi. The opportunity to trade stories and experiences across cities through a Zoom meeting is only possible in this WFH environment. What a great opportunity! I'm now setting aside a few hours each Friday to connect virtually with former colleagues both individually and in groups. While the atmosphere is not as enjoyable as sharing a glass of wine in a cute NYC venue, this ritual is still important and must evolve in the new world.

If you're the witness . . .

Don't gossip about who you've seen having drinks or dinner. That fuels the rumor mill and encourages everyone to view the meetings as somehow illicit and salacious. The effort to reframe the connections between male and female coworkers falls to all of us.

And those men who would be allies need to think about how a seemingly innocent request could be uncomfortable for a woman. Says Dawn:

> Here is a story I heard recently. "A male executive asked a female executive at a conference to come to his room to make a joint call to a client as there were no private spaces in the public area. She did and nothing inappropriate happened. But it was awkward. The boss should have rented a conference room or suggested they go to a quiet coffee shop or sit in a car."

CHAPTER 31

The Cellophane Standoff

Will men really starve rather than unwrap the danish tray?

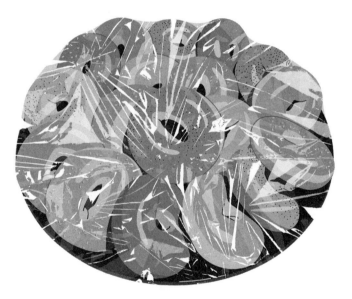

It's Bagel Tuesday and the platters have been delivered to the office. A full selection of carbs alongside tubs of cream cheese are all nicely arranged and wrapped in cellophane.

And there they will sit until a woman comes along to unwrap them.

We've seen this so many times we developed our own term—Cellophane Standoff—to describe it. The Cellophane Standoff is the unwavering obliviousness of our male colleagues when it comes to anything related to food service. They won't unwrap the bagels, unbox the sandwiches, or pass around the cookies. They'll go hungry first.

Why focus on this rather benign behavior? After all, it's not as if the men stand there and loudly demand a woman serve them. It's more a matter of neglect. They'll just avoid the chore rather than talk about who should handle it.

But we raise it because it's part of a larger office phenomenon. It's an example of the ways in which women are nudged towards doing the office housework.

Think about it: Who cleans up the coffee cups left in the sink? Who cuts and serves the cake at the office birthday parties? Who circulates the get-well card for an ill colleague? Anyone can handle these chores and in some offices, they are fairly distributed. But in most cases, office housework is handled by women.

We didn't always notice this. But once we saw it, it was undeniable. Says Katie:

> How many times have you been in a lunch meeting where the men get up and leave while a woman stays behind to clean up? Or the breakfast meeting where everyone sits around waiting for the cellophane to somehow magically be removed from the bagels? Or, God forbid, someone needs to put a spoon in the salad dressing. In most cases, that person is going to be a woman. I strongly believe that for women, doing the household tasks in the office is a trap. You are not reinforcing your image as a nice person. That only happens if you're a guy.

For every minute you stay behind to clean up, you are not on the phone with a client or you are missing the hallway "meeting after the meeting." You are not doing your job. I don't know how much thought I gave this for years, but as I got more senior and noticed the pattern it really bothered me.

Our Gen Z and millennial colleagues say that Cellophane Standoff continues into their generations. "They'll either sit there or not take the cellophane off properly. Probably just poke a hole at the top and dig out one bagel," said one.

The phenomenon is widespread enough to be studied by social scientists. A paper published in the *American Economic Review* calls office housework a task with "low promotability"—as in not something likely to show up on your review and get you promoted. When it comes to tasks in the office that everyone would rather someone else handle, women are:

- More likely to volunteer
- More likely to be asked to volunteer
- More likely to say yes when asked to volunteer

The problem, experts say, is that women (and men) are caught in a very old, sexist circle. Housework, such as serving food, is considered "women's work," she says. So, when housework-type chores crop up in an office environment, men and women revert to their cultural roles. Men were likely never schooled to step up and handle a housework chore, so they don't. Women, on the other hand, have been socialized to serve the food or clear the table, and they recreate that pattern learned at home in the office setting.

Cie builds on this point:

> Women may start doing office chores due to traditional cultural roles but I think "the need to be liked" plays into this too. No doubt a woman gets some acknowledgment for setting up a luncheon, planning the retirement barbecue, or buying the congratulations card and getting it signed. So, wanting to be seen as nice and helpful, the pattern continues and women continue to fill more and more of the tedious roles.

And to Katie's point, when a man does step up to unwrap the bagels, he's more likely to receive praise for it. A study in the *Journal of Applied Psychology* found that what researchers termed "work-related altruism" such as performing office housework is not only less optional for women, but men get more credit for performing it.

What to do?

If it's you . . .

Don't. Wash your own coffee cup and leave the others. Get up and leave the conference room with the guys after the meeting lets out. Katie does this, even though she has to fight the guilt of walking away from a mess. "It bugs me that I feel a little guilty walking out of the room, but I think that if you don't you only enable the situation to continue."

Share the love, says Lori.

> I'm a big snacker, so I love coming to a meeting and realizing there is food. I agree with Katie's point that women shouldn't always be unwrapping the bagel platters and taking

the lids off the cream cheese containers. I'd suggest that when you notice this work hasn't been done, put down your things at the table and say, "Jack, can you join me here getting the bagels ready before the client joins us in five minutes?" Or if you really feel like this task always falls to you, stand up as you leave the room and say, "I'm running to wash my hands so I can enjoy one of those delicious muffins. Can someone please unwrap the platters while I'm out; I can't remember whose turn it is to do that."

If you're the boss . . .

Be aware that office housework often falls to women. Be proactive and assign the chores in a gender-neutral way. If a woman has volunteered, ask a man to assist in the chore. Remember to dole out praise for office housework evenly.

If you're the witness . . .

Be aware of housework chores and who handles them. Step up and tackle the chores yourself—ask for help if you need it.

Build Your Own Band

And join ours!

We've dispensed a lot of advice in these pages—our own, the voices of experts, the words of our peers. And as we leave you, we offer one more tip: build your own Band of Sisters.

Throughout our work lives, as we've moved up the career ladder, cycled in and out of different companies, we have all found that our relationships are what gave us our power. Talent, skills, faith, and luck all play a role. But time and again, when we faced a challenge, we drew strength and support from people in our closest circle.

How can you build your own Band? You can start right now. Here are our best tips:

Katie says:

> Stay in touch with people! See what friendships emerge when you are no longer working together. Be a connector and put people together who can help each other when they need it. Be a good friend and colleague and look out for each other. When you find a group, get together on occasion. We had one group of women when I was at Pepsi and we made it a point to get together a couple of times a year for dinner. We're not in

touch as frequently now, but I know I could reach out to any of them at any time.

Lori says:

Make the time. It's so easy to cancel out of a lunch or dinner when you're tired and overworked. And yet, making the time makes the space to create the moments that really matter. And when you show up, really show up; get off your phone and be fully present. It's an overused thought, but it's true.

Always plan to give more than you get. Be generous of spirit in being there for others. Listen and be generous with your offers to help. Don't expect anything in return. Be generous with your time, your introductions, your sponsorship, and your wisdom.

Be a vault. Never *ever ever ever* betray a confidence.

Angelique says:

We were lucky to work at a place like PepsiCo that had so many talented female leaders who also became friends. However, you can collect a Band of Sisters from anywhere, and even one at a time. Introduce them to each other. If you have to, join a pre-fab group like Chief to find some sisters. Rent to buy! Start small, start slow, but definitely start!

Cie says:

Be easy to reach and 100 percent dependable.

Quickly respond to a call or a text whether to chitchat, brainstorm, make an introduction, or provide a reference.

I always talk to headhunters even if I am not interested in a job as I always have several folks who are in the job market that I want to get on their radar.

And finally, Ralph Waldo Emerson once said: "The only way to have a friend is to be one." To that end, I say: "The only way to have Sisters is to be one." We need to own the "I know a great gal" process and really advocate for other women.

Dawn says:

Keep up with former colleagues you valued as you move to new jobs. It is easy to get busy and not find time. But months and years later when you need their advice, you need them in your band, it may feel awkward. Just make time each month for a reconnect. And be strategic. Think about who you valued and who might be even more important in the future. Finally, think about whose band you could be a part of. Who do you want to help succeed and share your experience with? This can be very personally rewarding.

Mitzi says:

I highly recommend participating in a Band—whether

you join one or create one. I've grown from investing time and energy with a variety of Bands—some all-African American females, some women of color only, some in which I was the only female.

I encourage you to choose a Band or Bands where there is mutual benefit (not necessarily equal) from your participation and engagement. What I looked for and would suggest as a "must have" for everyone is a Band where you feel psychologically safe—to ask questions, to challenge, to brainstorm, to problem-solve, to vent, to explore, to grow, to be you.

The Bands that I have been a part of have been extremely beneficial in helping me grow and thrive professionally and personally. I am an advocate for having multiple mentors to learn from. I feel similarly about "Bands." From my Band of Sisters, to my PepsiCo multicultural Sistahs, to the Ragged 10 (a group of nine African American Male PepsiCo GMs plus one African American Sister—me), I am grateful for the Bands that I have been a part of and how the members have been instrumental in my development as a leader and in my life. Lastly, if being a part of a Band is your choice, be intentional in your pursuit of the Band for you. And when you find a good one, stay with it—the relationships you cultivate can be invaluable.

And while you're building your own Band, we invite you to come play along with ours.

TheBandOfSisters.com

SOURCES

Chapter 1

Diehl, Amy, and Leanne Dzubinski. "We Need to Stop 'Untitling' and 'Uncredentialing' Professional Women." *Fast Company*, January 21, 2021. https://www.fastcompany.com/90596628/we-need-to-stop-untitling-and-uncredentialing-professional-women.

Epstein, Joseph. "Is There a Doctor in the White House? Not if You Need an M.D." *The Wall Street Journal*, December 11, 2020. https://www.wsj.com/articles/is-there-a-doctor-in-the-white-house-not-if-you-need-an-m-d-11607727380.

Gaucher, Danielle, Justin Friesen, and Aaron C. Kay. "Evidence That Gendered Wording in Job Advertisements Exists and Sustains Gender Inequality." *Journal of Personality and Social Psychology* 101, no. 1 (2011): 109–28.

Liu, Deb. "The Right Words for the Job: How Gendered Language Affects the Workplace." *Medium: Women in Product*, February 25, 2017.

Stroi, O. (2020). Gender-Biased Language of the Workplace. Discourse. 5. 120-131. 10.32603/2412-8562-2019-5-6-120-131.

Chapter 2

Wang, Wendy. "Mothers and Work: What's 'Ideal'?" *Pew Research Center*, May 30, 2020.

Chapter 3

Bennett, Jessica. "I'm Not Mad. That's Just My RBF." *New York Times*, August 1, 2015. https://www.nytimes.com/2015/08/02/fashion/im-not-mad-thats-just-my-resting-b-face.html.

Dunlap, Kelley. "17 More Accurate Names for Resting Bitch Face." *BuzzFeed*,

June 23, 2015. https://www.buzzfeed.com/kelleydunlap/kacey-mus-graves-resting-bitch-face#.hwKbVQZGd

LaFrance, Marianne, Marvin A. Hecht, and Elizabeth Levy Paluck. "The Contingent Smile: A Meta-Analysis of Sex Differences in Smiling." *Psychological Bulletin* 129, no. 2 (March 2003): 305–34. https://doi.org/10.1037/0033-2909.129.2.305.

Thorpe, JR. "Why Do People Expect Women to Smile?" *Bustle*, July 6, 2017. https://www.bustle.com/p/why-do-people-expect-women-to-smile-67360.

Chapter 4

Quast, Lisa. "Ending Gender Bias: Why Richard Branson Says Everyone Should Take Meeting Notes, Not Just Women." *Forbes Magazine*, October 7, 2015. https://www.forbes.com/sites/lisaquast/2015/08/31/ending-gender-bias-why-richard-branson-says-everyone-should-take-meeting-notes-not-just-women/.

Williams, Joan C., and Marina Multhaup. "For Women and Minorities to Get Ahead, Managers Must Assign Work Fairly." *Harvard Business Review*, June 28, 2021. https://hbr.org/2018/03/for-women-and-minorities-to-get-ahead-managers-must-assign-work-fairly.

Chapter 5

AFSCME. "By the Numbers: Women Continue to Face Pregnancy Discrimination in the Workplace—an Analysis of U.S. Equal Employment Opportunity Commission Charges (Fiscal Years 2011-2015)." *AFSCME Information Highway*, October 31, 2016. http://www.afscmeinfocenter.org/blog/2016/10/by-the-numbers-women-continue-to-face-pregnancy-discrimination-in-the-workplace-an-analysis-of-u-s-equal-employment-opportunity-commission-charges-fiscal-years-2011-2015.htm.

Little, Laura M., Virginia Smith Major, Amanda S. Hinojosa, and Debra L. Nelson. "Professional Image Maintenance: How Women Navigate Pregnancy in the Workplace." *Academy of Management Journal* 58, no. 1 (2015): 8–37. https://doi.org/10.5465/amj.2013.0599.

Robinson, Bryan. "Pregnancy Discrimination in the Workplace Affects Mother and Baby Health." *Forbes Magazine*, July 11, 2020. https://www.forbes.com/sites/bryanrobinson/2020/07/11/pregnancy-discrimination-in-the-workplace-affects-mother-and-baby-health/.

Chapter 6

Cuddy, Amy J., Susan T. Fiske, and Peter Glick. "When Professionals Become Mothers, Warmth Doesn't Cut the Ice." *Journal of Social Issues* 60, no. 4 (December 1, 2004): 701–18. https://doi.org/10.1111/j.0022-4537.2004.00381.x.

Pearson, Allison. *I Don't Know How She Does It: The Life of Kate Reddy, Working Mother: A Novel.* New York: Anchor Books, 2011.

White, Rebecca. 2005. "I Do Know How She Does It (But Sometimes I Wish I Didn't)." William and Mary Journal of Women and Law 11, 2:209-20, https://scholarship.law.wm.edu/wmjowl/vol11/iss2/5.

Chapter 7

Elsesser, Kim. "Tokyo Olympics Head Thinks Women Talk Too Much— Research Says They Don't." *Forbes Magazine*, February 3, 2021. https://www.forbes.com/sites/kimelsesser/2021/02/03/tokyo-olympics-head-thinks-women-talk-too-much---research-says-they-dont/.

Heilman, Madeline E., and Michelle C. Haynes. "No Credit Where Credit Is Due: Attributional Rationalization of Women's Success in Male-Female Teams." *Journal of Applied Psychology* 90, no. 5 (2005): 905–16. https://doi.org/10.1037/0021-9010.90.5.905.

McClean, Elizabeth J., Sean R. Martin, Kyle J. Emich, and Col. Todd Woodruff. "The Social Consequences of Voice: An Examination of Voice Type and Gender on Status and Subsequent Leader Emergence." *Academy of Management Journal* 61, no. 5 (2018): 1869–91. https://doi.org/10.5465/amj.2016.0148.

Rich, Motoko, Hikari Hida, and Makiko Inoue. "Tokyo Olympics Chief Apologizes for Remarks Demeaning Women." *New York Times*,

February 3, 2021. https://www.nytimes.com/2021/02/03/sports/olym-pics/tokyo-olympics-yoshiro-mori.html.

"What Would You Do If You Weren't Afraid?" *Lean In*, May 27, 2013. https://www.youtube.com/watch?v=bAxQXZbhyvM.

Chapter 8

Castrillon, Caroline. "How Women Can Stop Apologizing and Take Their Power Back." *Forbes Magazine*, July 15, 2019. https://www.forbes.com/sites/carolinecastrillon/2019/07/14/how-women-can-stop-apologizing-and-take-their-power-back/.

Jacobson, Rae. "Why Girls Apologize Too Much." Child Mind Institute, September 7, 2021. https://childmind.org/article/why-girls-apologize-too-much/.

Reiss, Tami. "Just Not Sorry! (the backstory)." *Medium*, December 22, 2015. https://tamireiss.medium.com/just-not-sorry-the-backstory-33f54b30fe48.

Schumann, Karina, and Michael Ross. "Why Women Apologize More than Men." *Psychological Science* 21, no. 11 (2010): 1649–55. https://doi.org/10.1177/0956797610384150.

Chapter 9

Baldoni, John. "Will 'Upspeak' Hurt Your Career?" *Forbes Magazine*, July 26, 2018. https://www.forbes.com/sites/johnbaldoni/2015/07/30/will-up-speak-hurt-your-career/.

Green, Emma. "A Female Senator Explains Why Uptalk Is Part of Women's 'Nature.'" *The Atlantic*, January 16, 2014. https://www.theatlantic.com/politics/archive/2014/01/a-female-senator-explains-why-uptalk-is-part-of-womens-nature/283107/.

Maestas, Rica. "Explore Brown University." In Defense of Upspeak: Reclaiming "feminine" communication styles at work. Public Humanities. Brown University, 2019. https://www.brown.edu/academics/

public-humanities/blog/defense-upspeak-reclaiming-%E2%80%9Cfem-inine%E2%80%9D-communication-styles-work.

Peterson, Christopher. "Upspeak Makes Me Cringe." *Psychology Today*. Sussex Publishers, December 31, 2010. https://www.psychologytoday.com/us/blog/the-good-life/201012/upspeak.

Skorobogatov, Yana. "Robin T. Lakoff: 'What's up with Upspeak?'" Social Science Matrix, September 30, 2015. https://matrix.berkeley.edu/research-article/whats-upspeak/.

Chapter 10

Bleznak, Becca. "'The Devil Wears Prada': How Anna Wintour Showed Her 'Great Sense of Humor' about the Movie," June 14, 2021. https://www.cheatsheet.com/entertainmnt/the-devil-wears-prada-anna-wintour-showed-great-sense-humor-movie.html/.

Diaz, Daniella. "Trump calls Clinton 'a nasty woman,'" October 20, 2016. https://www.cnn.com/2016/10/19/politics/donald-trump-hillary-clinton-nasty-woman/index.html.

"For the Record: Obama Endorses Clinton as 'Likable Enough.'" *USA Today*, June 10, 2016. https://www.usatoday.com/story/news/politics/onpolitics/2016/06/10/record-obama-endorses-clinton-likable-enough/85675584/.

Gerhards, Leonie, and Michael Kosfeld. "I (Don't) Like You! but Who Cares? Gender Differences in Same-Sex and Mixed-Sex Teams." *The Economic Journal* 130, no. 627 (2020): 716–39. https://doi.org/10.1093/ej/uez067.

Kendall, Shari, and Deborah Tannen. "Gender and Language in the Workplace." *Gender and Discourse*, 1996, Chapter 4. https://doi.org/10.4135/9781446250204.n5.

Martin, Colette. "Women in the Workplace Are Just Too Nice." *Forbes Magazine*, August 9, 2011. https://www.forbes.com/sites/work-in-progress/2011/05/23/women-in-the-workplace-are-just-too-nice/.

Menendez, Alicia. *The Likeability Trap: How to Break Free and Succeed as You Are.* HarperBusiness, 2019.

"Sally Fields Acceptance Speech, Academy Awards Acceptance Speech Database, 1984." Academy of Motion Picture Arts & Sciences, March 25, 1985. http://aaspeechesdb.oscars.org/link/057-3/.

Chapter 11

Blanding, Michael. "The Surprising Benefits of Oversharing." HBS Working Knowledge, June 1, 2015. https://hbswk.hbs.edu/item/the-surprising-benefits-of-oversharing.

Brown, Brené. "The Power of Vulnerability." TEDxHouston, June 2010. https://www.ted.com/talks/brene_brown_the_power_of_vulnerability?language=en.

Gibson, Kerry Roberts, Dana Harari, and Jennifer Carson Marr. "When Sharing Hurts: How and Why Self-Disclosing Weakness Undermines the Task-Oriented Relationships of Higher Status Disclosers." *Organizational Behavior and Human Decision Processes* 144 (2018): 25–43. https://doi.org/10.1016/j.obhdp.2017.09.001.

Palmer, Erin. "LinkedIn Study: 67% of Millennial Employees Get Personal with Friends at Work." Businessadministrationinformation.com, July 11, 2014. https://www.businessadministrationinformation.com/news/linkedin-study-67-of-millennial-employees-get-personal-with-friends-at-work.

Chapter 12

Huhman, Heather R. "How to Be a Part of the Male Conversations at Work." *Forbes Magazine,* May 30, 2012. https://www.forbes.com/sites/work-in-progress/2012/05/30/how-to-be-a-part-of-the-male-conversations-at-work/.

Tannen, Deborah. *You Just Don't Understand: Women and Men in Conversation.* New York: William Morrow, 2013.

Chapter 13

Davies-Netzley, Sally Ann. "Women above the Glass Ceiling." *Gender & Society* 12, no. 3 (1998): 339–55. https://doi.org/10.1177/089124329801 2003006.

Kanter, Rosabeth Moss. "The Impact of Hierarchical Structures on the Work Behavior of Women and Men." *Social Problems* 23, no. 4 (1976): 415–30. https://doi.org/10.2307/799852.

Lyness, Karen S., and Donna E. Thompson. "Climbing the Corporate Ladder: Do Female and Male Executives Follow the Same Route?" *Journal of Applied Psychology* 85, no. 1 (2000): 86–101. https://doi. org/10.1037/0021-9010.85.1.86.

Chapter 14

Bennett, Jessica. "I'll Share My Salary Information If You Share Yours." *New York Times*, January 9, 2020. https://www.nytimes.com/2020/01/09/ style/women-salary-transparency.html.

Bleweis, Robin. "Quick Facts About the Gender Wage Gap." Center for American Progress, March 24, 2020. https://www.americanprogress.org/ issues/women/reports/2020/03/24/482141/quick-facts-gender-wage-gap/.

Brake, Deborah, and Joanna Grossman. "Title VII's Protection against Pay Discrimination." Hofstra University Center for the Study of Labor and Democracy, 2007. https://www.hofstra.edu/pdf/academics/colleges/ hclas/cld/cld_rlr_fall07_title7_grossman.pdf.

Brancaccio, David. "Can Talking about Salaries Reduce the Wage Gap?" *Marketplace*, June 7, 2019. https://www.marketplace.org/2019/06/07/ can-talking-about-salaries-reduce-the-wage-gap/.

Narula, Svati Kirsten. "How Much Do Millennials Make? They're More Than Happy to Tell You." *Wall Street Journal*, May 3, 2021. https://www.wsj. com/articles/how-money-much-do-millennials-make-theyre-more-than-happy-to-tell-you-11620061103.

Chapter 15

A. Allen, Joseph, Nale Lehmann-Willenbrock, and Nicole Landowski. "Linking Pre-Meeting Communication to Meeting Effectiveness." *Journal of Managerial Psychology* 29, no. 8 (2014): 1064–81. https://doi. org/10.1108/jmp-09-2012-0265.

Cavanaugh, Lynn Varacalli. "An important attribute of success is to be yourself. Never hide what makes you." "3 Steps to Take next Time You're Blindsided at Work." Progressive Women's Leadership, April 28, 2016. https://www.progressivewomensleadership.com/3-steps-to-take-next-time-youre-blindsided-at-work/.

Heath, Kathryn, Jill Flynn, and Mary David Holt. "Success on the Corporate Stage: Why Meetings Matter Even More for Women." https://flynnheath. com/wp-content/uploads/2016/01/Why-Meetings-Matter-Even-More-for-Women_FHH-Report_June-2014.pdf.

Chapter 16

Abouzahr, Katie, Matt Krentz, Claire Tracey, and Miki Tsusaka. "Dispelling the Myths of the Gender 'Ambition Gap.'" *BCG Global*, January 8, 2021. https://www.bcg.com/publications/2017/people-organization-leadership-change-dispelling-the-myths-of-the-gender-ambition-gap.

Tinsley, Catherine H., and Robin J. Ely. "What Most Companies Get Wrong about Men and Women." *Harvard Business Review*, November 19, 2019. https://hbr.org/2018/05/what-most-people-get-wrong-about-men-and-women.

Chapter 17

Sullivan-Hasson, Elizabeth. "TrustRadius 2021 Women in Tech Report," March 8, 2021. https://www.trustradius.com/buyer-blog/women-in-tech-report?utm_source=pr&utm_medium=pressrelease&utm_campaign=womenintech2021.

van Veelen, Ruth, Belle Derks, and Maaike Dorine Endedijk. "Double Trouble: How Being Outnumbered and Negatively Stereotyped Threatens

Career Outcomes of Women in STEM." *Frontiers in Psychology* 10 (2019). https://doi.org/10.3389/fpsyg.2019.00150.

"Women in the Workplace 2021." LeanIn.Org and McKinsey & Company. Accessed October 6, 2021. https://womenintheworkplace.com/.

Chapter 18

Mallya, Malavika. "How R and R Programs Impact the Two Genders: Empuls." *Empuls* (blog), August 10, 2021. https://blog.empuls.io/role-of-gender-in-r-r/.

Sittenthaler, Hanna M., and Alwine Mohnen. "Cash, Non-Cash, or Mix? Gender Matters! the Impact of Monetary, Non-Monetary, and Mixed Incentives on Performance." *Journal of Business Economics* 90, no. 8 (2020): 1253–84. https://doi.org/10.1007/s11573-020-00992-0.

Chapter 19

Green, Alison. "Our Traditionally Male Company Has an Annual Golf Trip—but Our New Female Employees Don't Play." *Ask a Manager*, December 7, 2019. https://www.askamanager.org/2019/12/most-popular-posts-of-2019-2.html.

Chapter 20

Hitlan, Robert T., Rebecca J Clifton, and M. Catherine DeSoto. "Perceived Exclusion in the Workplace: The Moderating Effects of Gender on Work Related Attitudes and Psychological Health." *North American Journal of Psychology* 8, no. 2 (2006): 217–36. "Office Cliques at Work: A Symptom of a Failed Diversity & Inclusion Strategy." *Prevue HR*, January 9, 2020. https://www.prevuehr.com/resources/insights/office-cliques-at-work-a-symptom-of-a-failed-diversity-inclusion-strategy/.

O'Reilly, Jane. "Is Negative Attention Better than No Attention? the Comparative Effects of Ostracism and Harassment at Work." *Organization Science*, April 4, 2014. https://pubsonline.informs.org/doi/abs/10.1287/orsc.2014.0900.

Chapter 21

Drexler, Peggy. "Navigating the Perils of Office Gossip." *Psychology Today*, February 27, 2104. https://www.psychologytoday.com/us/blog/our-gender-ourselves/201304/navigating-the-perils-office-gossip.

Farley, Sally D., Diane R. Timme, and Jason W. Hart. "On Coffee Talk and Break-Room Chatter: Perceptions of Women Who Gossip in the Workplace." *The Journal of Social Psychology* 150, no. 4 (2010): 361–68. https://doi.org/10.1080/00224540903365430.

Chapter 22

Cullen, Zoë B., and Ricardo Perez-Truglia. "The Old Boys' Club: Schmoozing and the Gender Gap." *NBER*, December 9, 2019. https://www.nber.org/papers/w26530.

Land, Ilene. "Co-Opt The Old Boys' Club: Make It Work for Women." *Harvard Business Review*, August 1, 2014. https://hbr.org/2011/11/co-opt-the-old-boys-club-make-it-work-for-women.

Chapter 23

Emily, Friedman. "Can Clinton's Emotions Get the Best Of Her?" *ABC News*, January 7, 2008. https://abcnews.go.com/Politics/Vote2008/story?id=4097786&page=1.

Fischer, Agneta H., Alice H. Eagly, and Suzanne Oosterwijk. "The Meaning of Tears: Which Sex Seems Emotional Depends on the Social Context." *European Journal of Social Psychology*, 2013. https://doi.org/10.1002/ejsp.1974.

Smith, Jacqueline S., Victoria L. Brescoll, and Erin L. Thomas. "Constrained by Emotion: Women, Leadership, and Expressing Emotion in the Workplace." *Handbook on Well-Being of Working Women*, 2016, 209–24. https://doi.org/10.1007/978-94-017-9897-6_13.

Chapter 24

Exley, Christine, and Judd Kessler. "The Gender Gap in Self-Promotion." *National Bureau of Economic Research Working Paper Series VL*, October 2019. https://doi.org/10.3386/w26345.

Mohr, Tara S. "Why Women Don't Apply for Jobs Unless They're 100% Qualified." *Harvard Business Review*, August 25, 2014. https://hbr.org/2014/08/why-women-dont-apply-for-jobs-unless-theyre-100-qualified.

Sandberg, Sheryl. *Lean in: Women, Work, and the Will to Lead.* 1st edition. New York: Alfred A. Knopf, 2013.

Tockey, Deanne, and Maria Ignatova. "Gender Insights Report: How Women Find Jobs Differently." LinkedIn Talent Solutions, 2019. https://business.linkedin.com/talent-solutions/resources/talent-strategy/gender-balance-report.

Chapter 25

Lucas, Brian Jeffrey, Zachariah Berry, Laura M. Giurge, and Dolly Chugh. "A Longer Shortlist Increases the Consideration of Female Candidates in Male-Dominant Domains," 2021, 736–42. https://doi.org/10.31219/osf.io/h7tnc.

Chapter 26

House, Jeremy. "How Faculty of Color Hurt Their Careers Helping Universities with Diversity." *Issues in Higher Education*, November 27, 2017. https://www.diverseeducation.com/home/article/15101692/how-faculty-of-color-hurt-their-careers-helping-universities-with-diversity.

Chapter 27

Abbott, Ida. "High Quality Mentoring and Sponsorship Can Increase Diversity and Inclusion." Ida Abbott Consulting LLC, October 2018. https://idaabbott.com/articles/high-quality-mentoring-and-sponsorship-can-increase-diversity-and-inclusion/.

Ayyala, Manasa S., Kimberly Skarupski, Joann N. Bodurtha, Marlís González-Fernández, Lisa E. Ishii, Barbara Fivush, and Rachel B. Levine. "Mentorship Is Not Enough." *Academic Medicine* 94, no. 1 (2019): 94–100. https://doi.org/10.1097/acm.0000000000002398.

Foust-Cummings, Heather, Sarah Dinolfo, and Jennifer Kohler. "Sponsoring Women to Success (Report)." *Catalyst*, June 17, 2011. https://www.catalyst.org/research/sponsoring-women-to-success/.

Chapter 28

Dardenne, Benoit, Muriel Dumont, and Thierry Bollier. "Insidious Dangers of Benevolent Sexism: Consequences for Women's Performance." *Journal of Personality and Social Psychology* 93, no. 5 (2007): 764–79. https://doi.org/10.1037/0022-3514.93.5.764.

Glick, Peter, and Susan T. Fiske. "An Ambivalent Alliance: Hostile and Benevolent Sexism as Complementary Justifications for Gender Inequality." *American Psychologist* 56, no. 2 (2001): 109–18. https://doi.org/10.1037/0003-066x.56.2.109.

Chapter 29

Gatica-Perez, Daniel. "Automatic Nonverbal Analysis of Social Interaction in Small Groups: A Review." *Image and Vision Computing* 27, no. 12 (2009): 1775–87. https://doi.org/10.1016/j.imavis.2009.01.004.

Koch, Sabine C., Christina G. Baehne, Lenelis Kruse, Friederike Zimmermann, and Joerg Zumbach. "Visual Dominance and Visual Egalitarianism: Individual and Group-Level Influences of Sex and Status in Group Interactions." *Journal of Nonverbal Behavior* 34, no. 3 (2010): 137–53. https://doi.org/10.1007/s10919-010-0088-8.

Nelson, Audrey. "The Politics of Eye Contact: A Gender Perspective." *Psychology Today*, September 15, 2010. https://www.psychologytoday.com/us/blog/he-speaks-she-speaks/201009/the-politics-eye-contact-gender-perspective.

Chapter 30

McGinley, Ann C. "#MeToo Backlash or Simply Common Sense?: It's Complicated." Scholarly Commons @ UNLV Boyd Law, 2020. https://scholars.law.unlv.edu/facpub/1310/.

Chapter 31

Babcock, Linda, Maria P. Recalde, Lise Vesterlund, and Laurie Weingart. "Gender Differences in Accepting and Receiving Requests for Tasks with Low Promotability." *American Economic Review* 107, no. 3 (2017): 714–47. https://doi.org/10.1257/aer.20141734.

Heilman, Madeline E., and Julie J. Chen. "Same Behavior, Different Consequences: Reactions to Men's and Women's Altruistic Citizenship Behavior." *Journal of Applied Psychology* 90, no. 3 (2005): 431–41. https://doi.org/10.1037/0021-9010.90.3.431.

ACKNOWLEDGMENTS

If there's anything a text by six authors demonstrates, it's that it takes a team to create a great book.

We have many people to thank.

As a group, we'd like first and foremost to thank our colleagues at PepsiCo. The years spent working with you created the foundation for our Band of Sisters, this book, and so much more. In particular we'd like to highlight former chairmen and CEOs of PepsiCo, Indra Nooyi and Steve Reinemund, for their leadership and for creating an inclusive culture that enabled us each to thrive.

We'd also like to thank the many friends and colleagues who have continued to support and inspire us as we fanned out into the world to conquer new challenges. The list of people is far too long to list here and our gratitude is endless.

A special thank-you to the colleagues and associates who shared their stories with us. Your contributions helped us to show that gender bias in the workplace is a real and present issue. We are grateful to you for your candor and your trust in us.

We'd also like to thank the team that came together to help us put our experiences and vision into book form. Thank you to David Wilk at City Point Press and his team including Jeremy Townsend for copy editing and Barbara Aronica-Buck for book and cover design. Many thanks to our collaborating writer Ellen Neuborne and research assistant Leslie Landis. Thank you to our illustrator Max Schwear for his brilliant illustrations and to our photographer John DeMato.

We appreciate the efforts of our marketing and publicity team, anchored by Alicia Simons, in helping to get this book from our hands to yours. Thank you also to our friend and honorary "sister," Amy Radin (author of *The Change Maker's Playbook*) who selflessly shared so much of her writing and speaking journey with us.

Finally, while we worked as a team to write this book, we'll separate now to deliver our own personal thank-yous:

Dawn

I want to thank all my coworkers and bosses across so many great companies who helped me navigate my career, offered support at critical times, and made working fun. I thank my husband, Bruce Beach, who gave me my first job opportunity in business and truly was my mentor and advocate. And my parents, Kenneth and Nancy Hudson, who raised me to believe I could achieve whatever I worked hard at with no regard to gender.

Angelique

Thank you to my husband, David, for being a true ally as "lead parent" in our house for the past few years so I could stay in the workplace. Equally to my daughter, Sophia, and son, George, who motivate me every day to be the best working mom I can be, and to my parents and sister who first taught me how awesome a trusted network feels.

Katie

Thank you to my husband, David Berson, for his enthusiasm, support, and patience throughout . . . and for his diligence in getting up at 4 a.m. to read chapters before work. You are my "proof of concept" that there are good men who want to be allies. I am truly fortunate to have had parents and six siblings who have supported and encouraged me my entire life. And thank you to the young women in my life—Sally, Kate, Fiona, and Charlotte. You impress and inspire me every day with your accomplishment and potential and are the reasons we need to do this work.

Lori

Thanks to my husband, James Marcus, and my daughters, Olivia and Sami, who patiently talked through every scenario in this book with me and didn't roll their eyes at me when I told the same stories over and over to anyone who said, "Oh . . . tell me about your book, Lori." I also want to thank my parents, the late Rose and Al Tauber, who raised my sister and me to be strong, independent women.

Cie

Thanks to my partner, Susan, who put up with overhearing countless Band of Sisters Zoom meetings, Zoom interviews, and being completely supportive during the entire writing process. And thank you to my 92-year-old mother who lives in my building sixteen floors above me, and weighed in daily. Virginia is my biggest fan and her never-ending support is a huge gift.

Mitzi

Thank you to my brothers, Mark and Montague, and their incredible wives, Angela and Terrilynn, for your unwavering love and support, and for sharing your stories and listening to mine during the writing of this book and always. To my nephews: Marcus, Marshawn, Malcolm, and Langston—I'm so proud of you and encouraged by the promise you demonstrate as the next generation of allies. I am grateful to my parents, the late Cozine and Robert Short, for modelling the way and preparing me for life's journey. Blessings to the many women who have poured into my life.